How to Get Rid of "it"

Before "it" Gets Rid of You

Topical Handbook for Healing & Deliverance Through Biblical Counseling

A Practical Self-Help Guide to Spiritual and Personal Growth

A series of easy spiritual exercises, interactive tools,
And step-by-step instructions to receive
Freedom from bondage
And experience spiritual healing and deliverance

Volume Twelve

ISBN-13: 978-1986462853

ISBN-10: 1986462854

How to Get Rid of "it"

Before "it" Gets Rid of You

Topical Handbook for
Healing and Deliverance
Through Biblical Counseling

A Practical Self-Help Guide to
Spiritual and Personal Growth

A series of easy spiritual exercises, interactive tools,
And step-by-step instructions to receive
Freedom from bondage
And experience spiritual healing and deliverance

Volume Twelve

Compilations of Works
By
Dr. Paulette Douglas

DEDICATION

**This book is dedicated to my Loving,
Supportive, Faithful Children, Step-Children, Grand-Children, God Children and God-
Grand-Children**

**They inspirer me to be the Women that God has ordained me to be and to continue to
minister to God's people and to make full proof of my ministry**

CONTENT
How to Get Rid of "it", Before "it" Gets Rid of You

PREFACE

How to Get Rid of "it", Before "it" Gets Rid of You is a Deliverance and Spiritual Warfare Manual compiled by Dr. Paulette Douglas which is worth reading and re-reading more than once, in order to empower the reader when confronting personal crisis and trials. Dr. Paulette Douglas has compiled many practical, spiritual books bringing light to the evil that exists. She brings the deliverance ministry to the forefront, explaining how each and every believer can counteract evil and the devil. Not many believers understand the concept of the Holy Spirit and that we are all called to fight against the devil, our enemy. Dr. Paulette Douglas presents scriptural background and Bible passages from the old and new testaments, as well as prayers to share with the reader that each of us is called to resist and fight against the devil with the power of the Holy Spirit. Dr. Paulette Douglas refers to this as the deliverance ministry and explains this is one of the privileges all believers have at our disposal.

This background scripture material is necessary as many readers may be unfamiliar with these spiritual concepts. The main focus on the book is to be a manual; or one stop guide to show the reader what the bible has to say about deliverance as well as to expose the works and deceptions of the devil as well. The cover itself might seem an actual handbook- yet this book is truly a manual for deliverance. This exhaustive book contains too much information to be digested in a single, quick reading. The words contained are life changing. While some traditional readers and those in organized religion may find this book difficult to believe and a bit theatrical, a close-minded attitude is exactly what the devil wants in order to operate.

It is important to keep in mind the charismatic background of Dr. Paulette Douglas is based on the belief of the real workings of the Holy Spirit and the literal belief in modern day spiritual gifts such as tongues and healing. Much of the book is an invaluable resource where Dr. Douglas has taken scriptural truths and prayers and relates them to the modern-day believer to use and apply when facing any trial or work from the enemy. The scriptural references will empower any reader with a quick resource of how to respond in faith to any difficulty- large and small. It is a spiritual self-help book in the fact that it will allow the reader the tools to look within himself/her-self and identify any areas or issues where Satan has his foothold. Not only that it tells the reader how to face and address these issues! For those who are at a loss of how to begin to approach their spiritual problems there are a number of sample prayers applicable to any number of situations. The reader will get the impression as if this book was written for his or her own situation. This is a book to meditate on and use- and is not intended to collect dust on a book shelf. There are eleven sequels to this handbook which address many other issues that just might cover your "it".

In this twelve-book series, How to Get Rid of "it" Before "it" gets Rid of You we discuss evil spirits and how they operate:
1. The Apostolic anointing and ministry
2. How demons enter and oppress people
3. Curses and how to deal with them

4. Breaking bondages
5. Casting out spirits
6. Healing the wounded heart
7. Ungodly beliefs
8. Ministering to people
9. House cleansing
10. Discerning of spirits

What is "it"?

We are all created with a basic need to be loved. God created us to both give and receive love, but though damaged emotions, our capacity to receive love can be dramatically hindered. Ignorance of God's love will also hinder us from receiving the great and glorious love that He has for us. **The root of most "its" is a lack of love being received by that person.** Many of us have been damaged emotionally by rejection, abandonment, abuse, etc., and thereby our capacity to receive love has been reduced. **Only an emotionally healthy person is capable of both giving and receiving love as God intended.**

Self-worth issues can hinder love

Self-worth issues are rooted in believing that we are not worthy or deserve to be loved. When we believe that we are unlovable, we will unconsciously reject any love that comes our way. We won't believe the love, because we believe in our hearts that we are not worthy. **Self-worth issues are all rooted in our failing to see who we really are in Christ.**

If you walked into a gallery of world-class art, and pointed to a painting, saying, "That is the ugliest thing I've ever seen! Who painted that??" Now let's say the artist was standing right next to you. How do you think that would make him feel? Do you realize we are the artwork of God, a special painting crafted together by the master painter? Do you think it brings Him honor when we look down on ourselves? **We need to stop putting down what God has made.**

Many times, we have self-unforgiveness issues because we blame ourselves for something, or we've done something we deeply regret, and we simply cannot let it go. We need to realize that Jesus has forgiven us of all our failures, and we need to start seeing ourselves as forgiven. Otherwise, we're denying the work of Christ in our life!

If God forgave you, and you're still beating yourself up, then you don't really believe what Jesus did for you. It's that simple!

Just as we must forgive others (see Matthew 18:21-35), we need to forgive ourselves just the same. Self-hate has been known to be the root behind diseases such as lupus and Crohn's disease, as well as other auto-immune diseases. We need to stop holding ourselves accountable for that which Jesus has set us free from.

If we want to be in faith, we need to BELIEVE what Jesus did for us, and part of that believing is seeing ourselves as forgiven and clothed with the righteousness of God, which is upon all who believe in the finished work of Christ. Without faith, it is impossible to please God (see Hebrews 11:6), so if you want to please God, start taking the finished work of the cross seriously, and begin to see yourself as forgiven, washed clean, and clothed in the righteousness of God. For the righteousness (right standing with God) is upon all who believe:

> *"Even the righteousness of God which is by faith of Jesus Christ unto all and upon all them that believe..." (Romans 3:22 KJV)*

Unforgiveness is rooted in a lack of realization of how much God has forgiven us, and therefore we're not thankful for the steep and terrible price that Jesus paid for our own failures. Therefore, it is so important to mediate on what Jesus did for us, until it transforms our heart. The message of Jesus' work for us is what causes faith to arise in our hearts and transforms us from the inside out (read Romans 10:8-17).

Learning to see yourself as God sees you, and forgive yourself because you want to please God and be in faith and be thankful for what Jesus did for you, is the biggest step in overcoming self-worth issues. Of course, there are spirits that may need to be driven out as well, such as self-hate, guilt, condemnation, etc.

Receiving the love God has for us

When it comes to God's love for us, that's obvious, considering how He loves even the sinner so much that Jesus came to die for them. Anybody who knows the message of the cross, has some knowledge of God's love for us. However, many times, we blame God for our problems, and so we don't believe the love that He has for us. Not only do we blame Him for our problems, many times we think that God gave us the sickness or problem in our life to teach us something. Nothing could be further from the truth! Jesus tells us clearly who came to kill, steal, and destroy, and who came so that we could have life and have it in abundance.

If we are going to receive the love that God has for us, we need to get our thinking straightened out. He's not the one behind our problems, but rather Jesus paid the full price so that we can be forgiven all our sins, both physically and emotionally healed, and blessed.

Look at how good God's heart is toward mankind! Not only did Jesus heal them, but He proved the blessings of the covenant we have with Him today concerning our healing and deliverance. Isn't He good toward us? **The reason why things happen to us, is because we live in a fallen world that is under the control of the evil one.** It's not God's fault. He loves you. Jesus died for you.

Settling the fact that God loves you and is good toward you is crucial to restoring your God-given capacity to receive His love. If you can't receive His love, then you need to stop and ask yourself four questions:

1. Am I blaming God for anything bad that happened to me?

2. Have I been emotionally wounded in such a way that it is hindering my ability to freely receive love as God intended me to?

3. Do I have knowledge and revelation of how much God loves me? Do I have a solid Biblical understanding of how I am loved with the same kind of love that the Father has for Jesus?

4. Is there a self-worth issue that makes me feel unworthy to be loved?

Settling these issues lays a foundation for breaking free from the power of the "IT". You must repair the damage and faulty thinking which hinders your ability to receive the love that God has for you.

How do you know if you are receiving God's love or if it's hindered? **If you are not passionate about Jesus, then somewhere your ability to receive His love is hindered.**

If you are living a life without receiving God's love in your heart daily, you are missing out on the most fulfilling life you can have here on this earth. To know God's love, which surpasses all understanding (see Philippians 4:7), dispels all our fears and gives us a sense of peace and joy that we could never otherwise know.

> *"And we have known and believed the love that God hath to us. God is love; and he that dwelleth in love dwelleth in God, and God in him. Herein is our love made perfect, that we may have boldness in the day of judgment: because as he is, so are we in this world. There is no fear in love; but perfect love casteth out fear: because fear hath torment. He that feareth is not made perfect in love." (1 John 4:16-18 KJV)*

What exactly is "it'?

An "it" is formed when we try to use something other than God, to meet our need to be loved. When our ability to receive God's love into our hearts is hindered, we will feel like something is missing, and seek to fill that void with something else. When that thing, whatever it might be, fills that void, we grow to love "it" because it's meeting a need. Over time, we establish a relationship with that thing, and when it comes time to depart, it's like breaking up a relationship. That's why the "it" is so destructive; we've relied on that thing to meet a need and we've established a relationship with it. Now when it's time to break up the love, it isn't so easy to say goodbye.

One widespread problem that we see when we try to deal with "it", is where we give up one "it" successfully, only to find yourself with another "it". We might quit drinking only to start overeating, for example. We might think we're finding victory, but all we're really doing is trading one "it" for another "it". This is because something must fill the love-void in our hearts, and if it's not one thing, it will be another.

What about cutting or self-harm?

Cutting or self-mutation is a special type of "it", where there's a need to either release pain in a person's heart or the person believes that they deserve to be punished for their failures. In these cases, the person certainly has an issue receiving the love that God has for them but there's another type of root that needs to be addressed as well. There's emotional pain or guilt that the person is dealing with that needs to be resolved. Finding out what happened and receiving Christ's truth concerning those areas is important for their healing. Any bondage involving guilt will need to be resolved through realizing and accepting the work of Christ on the cross for that person and they will likely need spirits of guilt, condemnation, self-hate, etc. driven out in Jesus' name. Again, getting the person to see them self for who they really are in Christ, forgiven, loved, and blessed, is crucial to lasting freedom from self-hate issues.

See yourself as lovable!

The key in uprooting most "its" is to deal with the underlying issues which are limiting their capacity to freely receive love from God and others, along with dealing with any self-worth issues by establishing an understanding of your true identity in Christ. **Coming to a place where you believe you are lovable is key to receiving love in general**, so dealing with self-worth issues is an important key to breaking down the walls which keep us from feeling loved. The only way to obtain a true sense of worth and value is to get a revelation of how much you are loved by God, who sent His son Jesus to die for you.

Discovering the root

To discover the root of your "it", you need to get real honest with yourself. Many times, we are in denial about the pain we are feeling. Figuring out what is the root of a bondage is all about asking the right questions, and that is especially important when it comes to uprooting an "it". Why don't we feel loved? Do we feel unlovable? (Let's stop right there; if we feel unlovable, then you've just discovered a self-worth issue that will need to be addressed.) Are you passionate about Jesus? If not, then something in hindering you from realizing how much you are loved by Him who died for you. Do you see yourself as forgiven and loved by the God because of what He did for you?

As you discover emotional wounds, you'll need to forgive (others, yourself, and God) and invite Jesus to come and heal the damage in your heart. If you don't realize how much God loves you, then you'll need to spend some time learning about what Jesus did for you on the cross, and what a terrible price He paid because He loved you so very much. Often breaking out of an "it" is a combination of emotional healing, learning about who you are in Christ, forgiving (yourself, others, and God), overcoming self-worth issues by changing how you see yourself (in light of how God sees and loves you), and casting out any spirits that came in and are enforcing the destructive behavior. Spirits behind guilt, condemnation, etc. also need to be driven out, as they seek to keep us from fully seeing what Jesus did for us on the cross.

Dealing with the issues underlying an "it" is key to uprooting it permanently. If you want lasting freedom and wholeness in this area of your life, you will have to deal with the issues that have limited your capacity to receive love, especially the love that God has for you.

"It Is Finished"
The Words of Victory

"When Jesus therefore had received the vinegar, he said, "It is finished.""—John 19:30
Words of triumph. In His words, "My God, my God, why hast thou forsaken me?" we heard the Savior's cry of desolation. In His words, "I thirst" we listened to His cry of lamentation. Now there falls upon our ears His cry of jubilation— "It is finished." From the words of the victim we turn now to the words of the Victor. The Cross of Christ has two great sides to it: it showed the profound depths of His humiliation, but it also marked the goal of the Incarnation, and further, it told the consummation of His mission, and it forms the basis of our salvation.

It is finished." What is found in these three words, "It is finished" is wrapped up the Gospel of God. In these words, contained the ground of the believer's assurance. In those words, is discovered the sum of all joy, and the very spirit of all divine consolation. Every" it" that we could ever encounter in our lives was dealt with on the cross therefore; we have the victory through Jesus Christ over any and every "it".

"It is finished." This was not the despairing cry of a helpless martyr. It was not an expression of satisfaction that the termination of His sufferings was now reached. It was not the last gasp of a worn-out life. No, rather was it the declaration on the part of the divine Redeemer that all for which He came from heaven to earth to do, was now done; that all that was needed to reveal the full character of God had now been accomplished; that all that was required by the Law before sinners could be saved, had now been performed—that the full price of our redemption was now paid.

"It is finished." The great purpose of God in the history of man was now accomplished—from the beginning, God's purpose has always been one and indivisible. It had been declared to men in numerous ways: in symbol and type, by mysterious hints and by plain intimations, through Messianic prediction and through didactic declaration. That purpose of God may be summarized thus: to display His grace in the creating of children in His own image and glory. And at the Cross the foundation was laid which was to make this possible and actual.

"It is finished." What was finished? The answer to this question is a very full one, though many excellent expositors have sought to limit the scope of these words and to confine them strictly to a single application. We are told it was the prophecies concerning the sufferings of Jesus which were finished, and that He referred only to this. It is readily granted that the immediate reference was to the Messianic predictions, yet we think there are good and sufficient reasons for not confining our Lord's words here to them. Yea, to us it seems certain that Christ referred specially to His sacrificial work, for all Scripture concerning His suffering and shame was not yet fulfilled. There remained the dismissal of His spirit into the hands of the Father (Psa 31:5); there remained the "piercing" with the spear (Zec 12:10: and note that the word used in Psalm 22:16 for the piercing of His hands and feet—the act of crucifixion—is a different one); there still remained the preserving of His bones unbroken (Psa 34:20), and the burial in the rich man's grave (Isa 53:9).

"It is finished." What was finished? We answer His sacrificial work. It is true there yet remained the act of death itself, which was necessary for the making of atonement. But, as is so often the case here in John's Gospel wherein our text is found (cf. Joh 12:23, 31; 13:31; 16:5; 17:4), the Lord here speaks of the completion of His work. Moreover, it must be remembered that the three hours darkness was already past, the awful cup had already been drained, His precious blood had already been shed, the outpoured wrath of God had already been endured; and these are the primary elements in the making of propitiation. The sacrificial work of Jesus, then, was completed, excepting only the act of death which followed immediately. But, as we shall see, the completing of the sacrificial work made an end of several things.

"It is finished."
1. Here we see the accomplished fulfillment of all the prophecies which had been written of Him here He should die. This is the immediate thought of the context: "When Jesus therefore had received the vinegar, He said, It is finished" (John 19:30). Centuries beforehand, the prophets of God had described step by step the humiliation and suffering which the coming Savior should undergo. One by one these had been fulfilled, wonderfully fulfilled, fulfilled to the very letter. Had prophecy declared that He should be the "woman's seed" (Gen 3:15), then He was "born of a woman" (Gal 4:4). Had prophecy announced that His mother should be a "virgin" (Isa 7:14), then was it literally fulfilled (Mat 1:18). Had prophecy revealed that He should be of the seed of Abraham (Gen 22:18), then mark its fulfillment (Mat 1:1). Had prophecy made it known that He

Prophecy said that He should be named before He was born (Isa 49:1), then so it came to pass (Luke 1:30-31). Had prophecy foretold that He should be born in Bethlehem of Judea (Mic 5:2), then mark how this very village was His birthplace. Had prophecy forewarned that His birth should entail sorrowing for others (Jer 31:15), then behold its tragic fulfillment (Mat 2:14-18). Had prophecy foreshown that the Messiah should appear before the scepter of tribal ascendancy had departed from Judah (Gen 49:10), then so He did, for though the ten tribes were in captivity, Judah was still in the land at the time of His advent. Had prophecy referred to the flight into Egypt and the subsequent return into Palestine, (Hose 11:1 and cf. Isa 49:3, 6), then so it came to pass (Mat 2:1415).

Prophecy made mention of one going before Christ to make ready His way (Mal 3:1), then see its fulfillment in the person of John the Baptist. Had prophecy made it known that at the Messiah's appearing "the eyes of the blind shall be opened, and the ears of the deaf shall be unstopped, then shall the lame man leap as a hart, and the tongue of the dumb sing" (Isa 35:56), then read through the four Gospels and see how blessedly this proved true. Had prophecy spoken of Him as "poor and needy" (Psa 40:17, see beginning of Psalm), then behold Him not having where to lay His head. Had prophecy intimated that He should speak in "parables" (Psa 78:2), then such was frequently His method of teaching. Had prophecy depicted Him stilling the tempest (Psa

107:29), then this is exactly what He did. Had prophecy heralded His "triumphal entry" into Jerusalem (Zec 9:9), then so it came to pass!

Prophecy announced that His person should be despised (Isa 53:3), that He should be rejected by the Jews (Isa 8:14), that He should be "hated without a cause" (Psa 69:4), then sad to say, such was precisely the case. Had prophecy painted the whole picture of His degradation and crucifixion, then was it vividly reproduced. There had been the betrayal by a familiar friend, the forsaking by His disciples, the being led to the slaughter, the being taken to judgment, the appearing of false witnesses against Him, the refusal on His part to make defense, the establishing of His innocence, the unjust condemnation, the sentence of capital punishment passed upon Him, the literal piercing of His hands and feet, the being numbered with transgressors, the mockery of the crowd, the casting lots for His garments—all predicted centuries beforehand, and all fulfilled to the very letter. The last prophecy of all which remained here He committed His Spirit into the hands of His Father, had now been fulfilled. He cried "I thirst," and after the tendering of the vinegar and gall, all was now "accomplished"; and as the Lord Jesus reviewed the entire scope of the prophetic Word and saw its full realization, He cried,

"It is finished"!
It only remains for us to point out that as there was a complete set of prophecies which had to do with the first advent of Jesus, so also is there a complete set of prophecies which have to do with His second advent—the latter as definite, as personal, and as comprehensive in their scope as the former. As then we see the actual fulfillment of those which had to do with His first coming to the earth, we may look forward with absolute confidence and assurance to the fulfillment of those which have to do with His second coming. And, as we have seen that the former set of prophecies were fulfilled literally and personally, so also must we expect the latter set to be. To grant the literal fulfillment of the former, and then to seek to spiritualize and symbolize the latter, is not only grossly inconsistent and illogical, but is highly injurious to us and deeply dishonoring to God and to His Word.

"It is finished."
2. Here we see the completion of His sufferings. But what tongue or pen can describe the sufferings of Jesus? The anguish, physical, mental, and spiritual, which He endured! Appropriately was He designated "the man of sorrows": suffering at the hands of men, at the hands of Satan, and at the hands of God. Pain inflicted upon Him by enemies and friends alike. From the beginning He walked the shadows which the Cross cast His path. "I am afflicted and ready to die from my youth up" (Psa 88:15). What a light this throws on His earlier years! Who can say how much is contained in those words? For us, an impenetrable veil is cast over the future; none of us knows what a day may bring forth.

But Jesus knew the end from the beginning! One has only to read through the Gospels to learn how the awful Cross was ever before Him. At the marriage-feast of Cana, where all was gladness and merriment, He makes solemn reference to "his hour" not yet come. When Nicodemus interviewed Him at night, the Savior referred to the "lifting up of the Son of man." When James and John came to request from Him the two places of honor in His coming kingdom, He made mention of the "cup" which He had to drink, and of the "baptism" wherewith He must be baptized. When Peter confessed that He was the Christ, the Son of the living God, He turned to His disciples and began to show unto them "how that he must go unto Jerusalem, and suffer many things of the elders and chief priests and scribes, and be killed, and be raised again the third day" (Mat 16:21). When Moses and Elijah stood with Him on the Mount of Transfiguration, it was to speak of "his decease which he should accomplish at Jerusalem" (Luke 9:31).

If it is true we are quite unable to estimate the sufferings of Christ due to the anticipation of the Cross, still less can we fathom the dread reality itself. The physical sufferings were excruciating, but even this was as nothing compared with His anguish of soul. To a consideration of these sufferings we have already devoted several paragraphs in previous chapters, yet we make no apology in turning to them again. We cannot contemplate too often what Jesus endured to secure our salvation. The better we are acquainted with His sufferings, and the more frequently we meditate thereon, the warmer will be our love and the deeper our gratitude.
At last the closing hours have come. There had been the terrible experience in Gethsemane followed by the appearing before Caiaphas, before Pilate, before Herod, and back again before Pilate. There had been the scourging and mocking by the brutal soldiers; the journey to Calvary; the fastening of His hands and feet to the cruel tree. There had been the reviling of the priests, the crowd, and the two thieves crucified with Him.

There had been the awful cloud that hid from the Father's face, which wrung from Him the bitter cry, "My God, my God, why hast thou forsaken me?" There had been the parched lips which drew from Him the exclamation "I thirst." There had been the fearful conflict with the power of darkness as the serpent "bruised" His heel. But now the suffering is ended. The Lord has bruised Him; man, and Devil have done their worst. The cup has been drained. The awful storm of God's wrath has spent itself. The darkness is ended. The sword of divine justice is done. The wages of sin have been paid. The prophecies of His sufferings are all fulfilled. The Cross has been "endured." Divine holiness has been fully satisfied (Isa 53:11). With a cry of triumph—a loud cry, a cry which reverberated throughout the entire universe—Jesus exclaims, "It is finished." The shame, the suffering and agony, are past. Never again shall He experience pain. Never again shall He endure the contradiction of sinners against Himself. Never again shall He be in the hands of Satan. Never again shall the light of God's countenance be hidden from Him. Blessed be God, all that is finished! "It is finished."

Jesus is concerned in the work of Redemption: He was the One who came here to die for sinners. He is the One who now gives spiritual illumination and understanding, and guides into the truth. Before the Lord Jesus came to this earth, a definite work was committed to Him. In the volume of the book it was written of Him, and He came to do the recorded will of God. Even as a boy of twelve the "Father's business" was before His heart and occupied His attention. Again, in John 5:36 we find Him saying, "But I have greater witness than that of John: for the works which the Father hath given me to finish, the same works that I do." And on the last night before His death, in that wonderful high priestly prayer, we find Him saying, "I have glorified thee on the earth: I have finished the work which thou gavest me to do" (John 17:4).

The mission upon which God had sent His Son into the world was now accomplished. It was not actually finished till He breathed His last, but death was only an instant ahead, and in anticipation of it He cries "It is finished." The demanding work is done. The divinely-given task is performed. A work more honorable and momentous than ever entrusted to man or angels, has been completed. That for which He had left heaven's glory that for which He had taken upon Him the form of a servant, that for which He had remained upon earth for thirty-three years to do, was now consummated. Nothing remained to be added. The goal of the Incarnation is reached. With what joyous triumph must He here have viewed the costly work which, committed to Him, had now been perfected!
"It is finished." The mission upon which God had sent His Son into the world was accomplished. That which had been eternally purposed had come to pass. The plan of God had been fully carried out.

Because He is the Most High, God's will, cannot be thwarted. Because He is supreme, God's counsel must stand. Because He is almighty, God's purpose cannot be overthrown.
"But he is in one mind, and who can turn him? And what his soul desireth, even that he doeth" (Job 23:13). "I know that thou canst do everything, and that no thought can be withholding from thee" (Job 42:2). "But our God is in the heavens: He hath done whatsoever he hath pleased" (Psa 115:3). "There is no wisdom nor understanding nor counsel against the Lord" (Pro 21:30). "For the Lord of hosts hath purposed, and who shall disannul it? And His hand is stretched out, and who shall turn it back?" (Isa 14:27). "Remember the former things of old: for I am God, and there is none else; I am God, and there is none like me: Declaring the end from the beginning, and from ancient times the things that are not yet done, saying, My counsel shall stand, and I will do all my pleasure" (Isa 46:9-10). "And all the inhabitants of the earth are reputed as nothing: and he doeth according to his will in the army of heaven, and among the inhabitants of the earth: and none can stay his hand, or say unto him, What doest thou?" (Dan 4:35). And, in the triumphant cry of the Jesus— "It is finished"—we have a prophecy and pledge of the ultimate carrying out of God's plan completely. At the end of time, when everything is wound up, and God's purpose has been fully consummated, when everything has been done which He before determined should be done, then shall it be said again, "It is finished."

"It is finished."
4. Here we see the accomplishment of the Atonement. Above we have spoken of Christ reaching the goal of the Incarnation, and of the consummation of His mission to the earth; what that goal and mission was, the Scriptures plainly reveal. The Son of Man came here "to seek and to save that which was lost" (Luke 19:10). Christ Jesus came into the world "to save sinners" (1Ti 1:15). God sent forth His Son, born of a woman, "to redeem them that were under the law" (Gal 4:5). He was manifested "to take away our sins" (1Jo 3:5). And all this involved the Cross. The "lost" which He came to seek could only be found there—in the place of death and under the condemnation of God. Sinners could be "saved" only by One taking their place and bearing their

iniquities. They who were under the Law could be "redeemed" only by Another fulfilling its requirements and suffering its curse. Our sins could be "taken away" only by their being blotted out by the precious blood of Christ. The demands of justice must be met; the requirements of God's holiness must be satisfied; the awful debt we incurred must be paid. And on the Cross, this was done; done by none less than the Son of God; done perfectly; done once for all.

"It is finished."
That to which so many types looked forward, was now accomplished. A covering from sin and its shame, typified by the coats of skin with which the Lord God clothed our first parents, was now provided. The more excellent sacrifice, typified by Abel's lamb, had now been offered. A shelter from the storm of divine judgment, typified by the Ark of Noah, was now furnished. The only-begotten and well-beloved Son, typified by Abraham's offering up of Isaac, had already been placed upon the altar. A protection from the avenging angel, typified by the shed blood of the Passover-lamb, was now supplied. A cure from the serpent's bite, typified by the serpent of brass upon the pole, was now made ready for sinners. The providing of a life-giving fountain, typified by Moses striking the rock, was now affected.

"It is finished." The Greek word here, teleo, is translated variously in the New Testament. A glance at some of the different renderings in other passages will enable us to discern the fullness and finality of the term used by Jesus. In Matthew 11:1, teleo is rendered as follows, "When Jesus had made an end of commanding his twelve disciples, he departed thence." In Matthew 17:24 it is rendered, "They that received tribute money came to Peter, and said, Doth not your master pay tribute?" In Luke 2:39, it is rendered, "And when they had performed all things according to the Law of the Lord, they returned into Galilee." In Luke 18:31, it is rendered, "All things that are written by the prophets concerning the Son shall be accomplished."

"It is finished." He cried: it is "made an end of"; it is "paid"; it is "performed"; it is "accomplished." What was made an end of? —our sins and their guilt. What was "paid?"—the price of our redemption. What was "performed?"—the utmost requirements of the Law. What was "accomplished?"—the work which the Father had given Him to do. What was "finished?"— the making of atonement. God has furnished at least four proofs that Christ did finish the work which was given Him to do. First, in the rending of the veil, which showed that the way to God was now open. Second, in the raising of Christ from the dead, which evidenced that God had accepted His sacrifice. Third, the exaltation of Christ to His own right hand, which demonstrated the value of Christ's work and the Father's delight in His person. Fourth, the sending to earth of the Holy Spirit to apply the virtues and benefits of Christ's atoning death.

"It is finished." What was "finished?"—the work of atonement. What is the value of that to us? This: to the sinner, it is a message of glad tidings. All that a Holy God requires has been done. Nothing is left for the sinner to add. No works from us are demanded as the price of our salvation. All that is necessary for the sinner is to rest now by faith upon what Christ did. "The gift of God is eternal life through Jesus Christ our Lord" (Rom 6:23). To the believer, the knowledge that the atoning work of Christ is finished brings a sweet relief over against all the defects and imperfections of his services. There is nothing "finished" that we do: all our duties are imperfect. There is much of sin and vanity in the very best of our efforts, but the grand relief is that we are "complete" in Christ (Col 2:10)! Christ and His finished work are the ground of all our hopes. "It is finished."

5. Here we see the end of our sins. The sins of the believer, all of them, were transferred to the Jesus. As the Scripture says, "The Lord hath laid on him the iniquities of us all" (Isa 53:6). If then God laid my iniquities on Christ, they are no longer on me. Sin there is in me, for the old Adamic nature remains in the believer till death or till Christ's return, should He come before I die; but there is no sin on me. This distinction between sin in and sin on, is a vital one, and there should be little difficulty in apprehending it. If I were to say the judge passed sentence on a criminal, and that he is now under sentence of death, everyone would understand what I meant. In like manner, everyone out of Christ has the sentence of God's condemnation resting upon him. But when a sinner believes in the Lord Jesus, and receives Him as his Lord and Master, obey the salvation message according to (Acts 2:38-39) he is no longer "under condemnation"— sin is no longer on him, that is, the guilt, the condemnation, the penalty of sin, is no longer upon him. And why? Because Christ bore our sins in His own body on the tree (1Pe 2:24)—the guilt, condemnation, and penalty of our sins, was transferred to our substitute. Hence, because my sins were transferred to Christ, they are no more upon me.

This precious truth was strikingly illustrated in Old Testament times regarding Israel's annual Day of Atonement. On that day, Aaron, the high priest (a type of Christ), made satisfaction to God for the sins which Israel had committed during the previous year. The way this was done is described in Leviticus 16. Two goats were taken and presented before the Lord at the door of the tabernacle: this was before anything was done with them: it represented Christ being sent and presenting Himself, offering to come into this world and be the Savior of sinners. One of the goats was then taken and killed, and its blood was carried into the tabernacle, within the veil, into the Holy of Holies, and there it was sprinkled before and upon the mercy seat—foreshadowing Christ offering Himself as a sacrifice, to meet the demands of His justice and satisfy the requirements of His holiness.

Then we read that Aaron came out of the tabernacle and laid both his hands upon the head of the second (living) goat— signifying an act of identification by which Aaron is the representative of the whole nation, identified the people with it, acknowledging that its doom was what their sins merited, and which, today, corresponds with the hands of faith laying hold of Christ and identifying ourselves with Him in His Death. Having laid his hands on the head of the live goat, Aaron now confessed over him "all the iniquities of the children of Israel, and all their transgressions in all their sins, putting them upon the head of the goat" (Lev 16:21). Thus, were Israel's sins transferred to their substitute. Finally, we are told, "And the goat shall bear upon him all their iniquities unto a land not inhabited: and he shall let go the goat in the wilderness" (Lev 16:22). The goat bearing Israel's sins, was taken unto an uninhabited wilderness, and the people of God saw him and their sins no more! In type this was Christ taking our sins into that desolate land where God was not and there making an end of them. The Cross of Christ then is the grave of our sins!

"It is finished."
6. Here we see the fulfillment of the Law's requirements. "The law is holy, and the commandment holy, and just and good" (Rom 7:12). How could it be anything less when Jehovah Himself had framed and given it! The fault lay not in the Law but in man who, being depraved and sinful, could not keep it. Yet that Law must be kept, and kept by a man, so that the Law might be honored and magnified, and its giver vindicated. Therefore, we read, "For what the law could not do, in that it was weak through the flesh, God sending his own Son, in the likeness of sinful flesh, and for sin, condemned sin in the flesh: that the righteousness of the law might be fulfilled in [not by] us, who walk not after flesh, but after the Spirit" (Rom 8:3-4). The "weakness" here is that of fallen man. The sending forth of God's Son in the likeness of sin's flesh (Greek) refers to the Incarnation: as we read in another Scripture, "God sent forth his Son, born of a woman, born under the law, that he might redeem them that were under the law" (Gal 4:4-5 RV). Yes, the Jesus was born "under the law," born under it that He might keep it perfectly in thought, word, and deed. "Think not that I am come to destroy the law, or the prophets: I am not come to destroy, but to fulfill" (Mat 5:17); such was His claim.

But not only did Jesus keep the precepts of the Law, He also suffered its penalty and endured its curse. We had broken it, and taking our place, He must receive its just sentence. Having received its penalty and endured its curse, the demands of the Law are fully met, and justice is satisfied. Therefore, is it written of believers, "Christ hath redeemed us from the curse of the law, being made a curse for us" (Gal 3:13). And again, "For Christ is the end of the law for righteousness to everyone that believeth" (Rom 10:4). And yet again, "For ye are not under the law, but under grace" (Rom 6:14). "It is finished." "Free from the Law, Jesus hath bled, and there is remission, cursed by the law and bruised by the fall, Grace hath redeemed us once for all."

7. Here we see the destruction of Satan's power. See it by faith. The Cross sounded the death of the devil's power. To human appearances it looked like the moment of his greatest triumph, yet, it was the hour of his ultimate defeat. In view of the Cross Jesus declared, "Now is the judgment of this world: now shall the prince of this world be cast out" (Joh 12:31). It is true that Satan has not yet been chained and cast into the bottomless pit, nevertheless, sentence has been passed (though not yet executed); his doom is certain; and his power is already broken so far as believers are concerned.

For the Christian, the devil is a vanquished foe. He was defeated by Christ at the Cross— "that through death he might destroy him that had the power of death, that is, the devil" (Hebrew 2:14). Believers have already been "delivered from the power of darkness" and translated into the kingdom of God's dear Son (Col 1:13). Satan, then, should be treated as a defeated enemy. No longer has he any legitimate claim upon us. Once we were his lawful "captives"; but now God worketh in us both to will and to do of His good pleasure. All that we now must do is to "resist the devil," and the promise is, "he will flee from you" (James 4:7).

"It is finished." Here was the triumphant answer to the rage of man and the enmity of Satan. It tells of the perfect work which meets sin in the place of judgment. All was completed just as God would have it, just as the prophets had foretold, just as the Old Testament ceremonial had foreshadowed, just as divine holiness demanded, and just as sinners needed. How strikingly appropriate is this sixth Cross-utterance of Jesus found in John's Gospel—the Gospel which displays the glory of Christ's deity! He seals it with His own words, attesting it is complete, and giving it the all-sufficient sanction of His own approval. Jesus says, "It is finished"—who then dare doubt or question it.

"It is finished." Reader, do you believe it? or, are you trying to add something of your own to the finished work of Christ to secure the favor of God? All you must do is to accept the pardon which He purchased. God is satisfied with His work on the cross, why are not you? Sinner, the moment you believe Jesus' testimony that it is finished, that moment every sin you have committed is blotted out, and you stand accepted in Christ! O would you not like to possess the assurance that there is nothing between your soul and God? Would you not like to know that every sin had been atoned for and put away? Then believe what God's Word says about Christ's death. Rest not on your feelings and experiences but on the written Word. There is only one way of finding peace, deliverance, wholeness, salvation, victory over the "it" and that is through faith in the shed blood of Jesus the of Lamb God. It is time to "Get Rid of "it", Before "it" Gets Rid of You".

"It is finished." Do you really believe it? Or, are you endeavoring to add something of your own to it and thus merit the favor of God? By continuing to hold on and struggle, seeking other sources to deal with the "it" in your life, you are nullifying the finished work of Christ by your own miserable additions to it!". The Gospel of God's grace, and the finished work of Christ is sufficient for our souls to rest upon. In the pages of this book, God uses forceful object lessons and His Word to show you, "How to Get Rid of "it", before "it" Gets Rid of You". It is a grave mistake not to embrace the Word of God, and cast yourself by faith upon what Christ had done for you.

Victory was given to us by way of the cross. Whatever your "it" or "its" might be, "it" has come to kill, steal and destroy you. Make a conscious effort to explore this information given in this book and expose the enemy of your soul. Let's "Get Rid of "it". After all, "It is Finished"

CHAPTER ONE

How to deal with "it" Biblical Counseling

Our Old Testament tells us that Counseling issues has existed since time began. It was a dismal time in the lives of God's people that was described by the Prophet Jeremiah. The people were backslidden, they refused to repent, and they rejected the Word of the Lord. The conditions were so dire that death was preferred to life (Jeremiah 8).

In the midst of these tragic circumstances, significant questions are raised: *"Is there no balm in Gilead; is there no physician there? Why then is not the health of the daughter of my people recovered?" (Jeremiah 8:22).* Gilead was a region east of Jordan that was famous for its medicinal salve. The questions--applied spiritually--were seeking answers as to why there was no cure for a suffering people. Where was the balm? Where was the physician who would apply the cure? Why were God's people continuing to live in defeat and bondage? The Old Testament King Jehoshaphat raised a similar query: "Is there no prophet of the Lord?", he asked as he faced a tremendous challenge from enemy nations (2 Kings 3).

Similar questions are echoing around the world today. Why are so many believers in bondage to addictions, harmful emotions, and sinful practices? Is there no "balm in Gilead" to heal their wounds? Are there no "spiritual physicians" to apply the healing ointment of the Word of God? Is there no prophet of the Lord to speak the Word of Life that will set them free?

There is a desperate need for the ministry of what may be called prophetic counseling-- counseling that is wholly based upon the Holy Bible, the authoritative Word of God. We need counselors who believe that God means exactly what He says and that the Word has within it the inherent power to meet very need--spiritual, physical, mental, emotional, and financial.

We need men and women of God who will boldly declare, "Thus says the Lord" to a lost, hurting, and spiritually dying world. Where are the spiritual leaders who will counsel prophetically, speaking forth the Word of God in answer to human need? Where are those who, instead of referring people to secular professionals, believe God's declaration...

...so is my word that goes out from my mouth: It will not return to me empty, but will accomplish what I desire and achieve the purpose for which I sent it.
(Isaiah 55:11, NIV)

As born-again believers, we believe that the Bible reveals salvation through Jesus Christ as the only way to obtain forgiveness from sin and guarantee eternal life. If we are staking our eternal destiny on the promises of redemption and salvation, then why do we hesitate to believe God's Word concerning deliverance, healing, and miracles? Why do we seek something other than the scriptures for answers to our problems?

Many pastors and church leaders today are referring people to secular psychologists, counselors, and clinics instead of dispensing the life-changing Word of God that will meet every need-- spiritually, emotionally, mentally, and physically. God's command is not "refer my people", "institutionalize my people", or "put my people on medication". His Word is *"Comfort, comfort my people says your God" (Isaiah 40:1).*

SECULAR PSYCHOLOGY

Secular psychology studies behavior and attempts to meet the needs of hurting people through scientific methods and theories developed by observation, experimentation, and experience. While psychology can help someone understand their negative behavior and enable them to acknowledge their problems, such issues can only be properly dealt with in the life of a believer through application of scriptural principles.   How can an unbeliever, who does not acknowledge God or His Word, counsel a believer whose whole life and destiny is rooted in faith?

God declared: *"The wise will be put to shame; they will be dismayed and trapped. Since they have rejected the word of the Lord, what kind of wisdom do they have?" (Jeremiah 8:9).* Is this the kind of counsel that you, as a believer, want to seek? Is this the type of "professional help" that you want to refer your family, friends, or followers to receive?

Many basic tenets of psychology are at odds with the scriptures. For example, secular psychologists may say, "It will take a long time to deal with this problem. You need extended counseling." But that is not what we see in the Word of God. When Jesus spoke the prophetic Word of God to hurting people, they were immediately healed, delivered, saved, and set free. Jesus never referred anyone to a secular professional for help. He never told anyone it would take "extended counseling" to deal with their issues. The Word was spoken and--if the recipient responded positively to it--they were immediately made whole spiritually, mentally, physically, and emotionally.

Consider the case of the Gadarene man who was possessed by a legion of demons (Mark 5:1-20). A legion in the natural world at that time consisted of five to six thousand foot soldiers under Roman rule.   This man had mental issues so great that he lived in a graveyard! He had supernatural strength from a host of demonic spirits. He was alienated from society and engaged in self-destructive behavior--cutting himself. Jesus spoke eight words: "Come out of this man, you evil spirit!"--and this man's life was changed (Mark 5:8). No long-term counseling needed. No referral to a mental facility. Just eight powerful Words from the lips of the Master.

For another example, consider the psychological model of the stages of grief. In response to tragedies such as death, terrible accidents, terminal illness, etc., psychologists say you will pass through stages of grief that include denial, anger, bargaining, depression, and finally acceptance. They say these stages can occur in any order and last for varying lengths of time. But where does it say this in God's Word? Is not the Holy Spirit who is resident within us our Comforter, and can we not call upon Him to fulfill this purpose when we are faced with tragedies?

The Bible does indicate there is a time to mourn (Ecclesiastes 3:4), but the immediate mourning following a death or tragedy is not the same as prolonged grief. Jesus bore your sin and shame on the cross, so you do not have to bear them. He also bore your grief so you need not bear it:

Surely, He has borne our griefs and carried our sorrows; Yet we esteemed Him stricken, Smitten by God, and afflicted. But He was wounded for our transgressions, He was bruised for our iniquities; The chastisement for our peace was upon Him, And by His stripes we are healed. (Isaiah 53:4-5, NKJV)

So if Jesus bore your grief, just as He bore your sin and shame, why must you go through "stages"? Why must you continue to grieve months or even years after a tragedy or loss? Is there no spiritual "balm in Gilead" to heal your wounds (Jeremiah 8:22)? Does not the Bible say *"He heals the brokenhearted and binds up their wounds" (Psalm 147:3)*. Will you take God at His Word, or will you follow a psychological model that says you must go through stages of grief?

Secular psychologists also talk much about self-esteem, but there is a difference between self-esteem and Christ-centered esteem. It is not who you are, but rather who He is and what He can do in you and through you. Christ-centered esteem recognizes you are no longer who you were, and acknowledges who you are as a born-again believer. You are a child of God, forgiven and redeemed from sin, adopted into the family of God, and a joint-heir with Jesus Christ.

Secular psychologists claim that "the best predictor of future behavior is past behavior." For the biblical counselor and his counselee however, this is not true. God says: *"Forget the former things; do not dwell on the past. See, I am doing a new thing! Now it springs up; do you not perceive it?" (Isaiah 43:18-19)*.

Your past does not predict the future when you become a new creature in Christ because *"...if any man be in Christ, he is a new creature: old things are passed away; behold, all things are become new" (2 Corinthians 45:17, NKJV)*.

The goal of counseling is not a "patched up version" of the old person, rather it is a new creature in Christ. The purpose of biblical counseling is not for rehabilitation, rather the goal is transformation--total change:

Do not conform any longer to the pattern of this world, but be transformed by the renewing of your mind. Then you will be able to test and approve what God's will is-- his good, pleasing and perfect will. (Romans 12:2)

The "patterns of the world" in secular psychology do not bring transformation. Psychological theories and models cannot change people. Only God can change a person from the inside out, give them a new mind, a new heart, and make them a new creature in Christ.

A biblical counselor believes God has the answer to every problem--not secular psychology. We are not adversaries of secular psychology, but we simply believe relying on it for answers is denying the sufficiency of scripture to meet every need.

People with tremendous needs came to Jesus from Galilee, Judaea, and Jerusalem, and the power of the Lord was present to heal them physically, spiritually, mentally, and emotionally (Luke 5:17). That same power is resident within a biblical counselor who speaks the prophetic Word of God into the lives of those seeking help.

WORDS WITHOUT KNOWLEDGE

The Bible warns about walking in the counsel of the ungodly (Psalm 1:1). A true believer who is walking by faith cannot be helped spiritually by a person who has refused to acknowledge God. The psalmist declared:

The Lord bringeth the counsel of the heathen to nought: he maketh the devices of the people of none effect. The counsel of the Lord standeth forever, the thoughts of his heart to all generations. (Psalm 33:10-11, KJV)

Sometimes, even counselors who are believers don't get it right. Large sections of the book of Job are filled with advice given by Job's friends. Generally speaking, Eliphaz spoke from experience, Bildad spoke on the basis of human authority, and Zophar emphasized legalism. If you want a manual on how not to counsel someone who is suffering, the book of Job is it!

From their counseling we learn that not all advice is good advice, even that given by well-intentioned friends. We learn from Job's friends that we should not pass judgment on those who suffer. Rather than giving theological dissertations, we should share in their grief, provide comfort, and speak the Word of God into their lives. We must be willing to acknowledge that we do not have all the answers as to the depth or extent of their suffering (Deuteronomy 29:29).

Like Job's counselors, some people may know the Word but may misapply it because of their traditions, experiences, prejudices, or perceptions. These counselors are speaking "words without knowledge (Job 38:2). Only the scriptures, properly interpreted and applied, can bring healing and deliverance to a struggling soul.

The *New American Commentary* aptly summarizes the faults of Job's counselors:

"A review of the speeches of Job's associates shows that they were poor counselors. They failed in several ways: (1) They did not express any sympathy for Job in their speeches. (2) They did not pray for him. (3) They seemingly ignored Job's expressions of emotional and physical agony. (4) They talked too much and did not listen adequately. (5) They became defensive and argumentative. (6) They belittled rather than encouraged Job. (7) They assumed they knew the cause of Job's problems. (8) They stubbornly persisted in their views of Job's problems, even

when their ideas contradicted the facts. (9) They suggested an inappropriate solution to his problem. (10) They blamed Job and condemned him for expressing grief and frustration. Counselors today do well to be sure they do not fail in similar ways."

AN ANSWER FOR EVERY NEED

A biblical counselor believes that a person does not have to undergo years of therapy. We believe the Bible has the answer to every problem and, when acted upon, the scriptures will manifest true change in the life of the counselee. The only time factor involved in this process is the length of time it might take someone to accept and act upon God's Word.

At some point in scriptural counseling, a counselee must either accept or reject what God has to say regarding their problems. When the Word of God is rejected, no further progress can be made in terms of biblical counseling. How sad it is when we turn elsewhere for peace, comfort, and release from sin, guilt, grief, and shame when Jesus Christ suffered and died to secure these blessings for us.

Believers experience many of the same conflicts as unbelievers, but they also have additional spiritual conflicts between their new nature and the old nature (Galatians 5:17). Only biblical counseling can deal with these issues from a scriptural perspective and guide a believer in spiritual growth. This is not to discredit any valid contributions by the field of psychology to counseling. It is merely to establish that--as in the case of all secular data--these contributions must be viewed through the lens of scripture.

We serve Jesus Christ, the Wonderful Counselor who has promised that *"He heals the brokenhearted and binds up their wounds" (Psalm 147:3).* When Jesus returned to Heaven, He sent "another counselor" to be with us and dwell within us (John 14:16-18). Biblical counseling is simply learning to release the supernatural power of this resident Counselor through application of scriptural principles.

A DEFINITION OF BIBLICAL COUNSELING

Here is a definition of biblical counseling developed by and agreed upon by experts in the field of biblical counseling:

"Biblical counseling endeavors to build a relationship with another person in which God's work of change can thrive. It is therefore dependent on the Word of God, the work of the Holy Spirit and the grace of Jesus Christ. It seeks to build a contextualized understanding of the counselee (past and present) and will view that data through the lens of Scripture. The Biblical counselor rests in the knowledge that he is not the change agent, but a tool in the hands of the One who is. The biblical counselor does not ignore physical issues or emotional data, but seeks to integrate them into a holistic understanding of the person and where change needs to take place. The

biblical counselor is not adversarial in his relationship to the psychologies of his culture, but examines research and insights through the lens of Scripture. In his work with the counselee the biblical counselor always recognizes the sovereignty of God, the transformative grace of Christ, and the insight-giving and conviction-producing ministry of the Holy Spirit. In all of this the biblical counselor sees himself not as an isolated instrument of change, but one whose work is intimately connected to God's primary tool of change; the church, with all of its God-ordained, duties, structures and means of grace."

Biblical counseling relies upon the Word of God rather than theories that are rooted in a worldly, defective understanding of human nature (John 17:17). Any method worthy of the name "Christian counseling" must address the root problem of sin and present God's solution--the redemptive work of Christ and the sanctifying power of the Holy Spirit through the Word of God.

While there may be conditions that warrant legitimate medical treatment, biblical counselors reject the assumptions of the therapeutic culture that offers a pharmacological solution for every problem. Too often, medications only alleviate the symptoms and do not deal with the root causes of issues.

Unfortunately, some believers have lost confidence in the power of God's Word to change lives because they do not understand and know how to apply the scriptures. Others do not believe the Word actually works for them or they claim miracles are not for today. Such unbelief hinders the work of God in their lives (Matthew 13:58).

Reading the Bible and memorizing verses are good practices, but change will not occur unless the Word of God is understood, believed, and applied. Before the people of Nehemiah's day experienced a change of heart, Ezra read the Word of God and helped them understand it. They heard, understood, believed, and acted upon the Word, and then change resulted. A biblical counselor must share the scriptures, make certain they are understood, and then direct the counselee in the appropriate response.

Jesus told the Pharisees, *"...You are mistaken, not knowing the Scriptures nor the power of God"* *(Matthew 22:29, NKJV).* Biblical counseling combines the Word of God with the power of God to effect true change in the lives of hurting people.

Jesus said:

Come to Me, all you who labor and are heavy-laden and overburdened, and I will cause you to rest. [I will ease and relieve and refresh your souls.] Take My yoke upon you and learn of Me, for I am gentle (meek) and humble (lowly) in heart, and you will find rest (relief and ease and refreshment and recreation and blessed quiet) for your souls. (Matthew 11:28-29, AMP)

The appeal to come has not changed. Jesus is still calling hurting humanity to come, just as they are--with their burdens, addictions, issues, sins, and failures. He still offers rest, refreshment, and re-creation--new life--as we learn of Him.

Some professional chaplains are counseling in difficult situations where they are forbidden by their employer and/or by law to say things like "homosexuality is a sin," etc. In such delicate situations, establish with the counselee that the counsel you are providing is not an opinion that you formulated, but it is the Word of God, the Holy Bible. The counselee is seeking biblical counseling, that is what you are providing, and that is what your counsel is based upon. They must make their own personal decision to accept or reject God's Word.

CHAPTER TWO

How to deal with the "it" The Biblical Counselor

One of the names of Jesus is "Wonderful Counselor" (Isaiah 9:6). Jesus counseled prophetically while here on earth, speaking the truth of God's Word into the lives of those who came to Him seeking help.

Christ's ministry of counseling was limited geographically while He was on earth, and eventually it was limited by time when He returned to Heaven. Upon His departure from earth, however, Jesus promised to send another Counselor to fulfill this purpose in our lives:

And I will ask the Father, and he will give you another Counselor to be with you forever--the Spirit of truth. The world cannot accept him, because it neither sees him nor knows him. But you know him, for he lives with you and will be in you. (John 14:16-17)

The Holy Spirit is the biblical counselor without limits. He is not limited by time or distance, because He dwells within each true believer. He is not limited by knowledge because as part of the Trinity of God He is all-knowing. The Holy Spirit within you can provide proper counsel in times of need and give you the ability to counsel others biblically.

Many times believers turn to counselors before they turn to God for help. As a believer, you already have a resident Counselor and intercessor within you. The Holy Spirit is your Counselor, and Jesus is the intercessor between you and God (1 Timothy 2:5).   When a believer turns to the world for counsel, the question is similar to that raised by the Prophet Micah: *"Now why do you cry out aloud? Is there no king in you? Is your counselor perished?" (Micah 4:9, KJV).* Much counseling would be unnecessary if people would take their concerns to God first and search His Word for answers.

For a believer, the Holy Spirit is the true biblical counselor. The person providing guidance based on the Word of God is simply a facilitator, speaking forth the counsel of the Holy Spirit. Biblical counseling is the work of the Holy Spirit accomplished in believers and through believers--whether they are a professional counselor, minister, chaplain, or simply a born-again, Spirit-filled believer.

Biblical counselors must be led by the Holy Spirit. Counseling apart from the Word of God and the power of the Spirit is ineffective. At times, the Holy Spirit may direct you to say something different than what you planned. At other times, the Spirit may caution you to remain silent at the very moment you were going to speak.

If you remain sensitive to the Holy Spirit, He will direct you as to what to say regarding every issue. Jesus promised that in difficult situations you are not to *"...worry beforehand, or premeditate what you will speak. But whatever is given you in that hour, speak that; for it is not you who speak, but the Holy Spirit"* (Mark 13:11, NKJV).

The Holy Spirit makes you, as a believer, competent to counsel. The Apostle Paul told the Romans: *"Now I myself am confident concerning you, my brethren, that you also are full of goodness, filled with all knowledge, able also to admonish one another"* (Romans 15:14, NKJV).

No counselor can know the truth about situations without supernatural revelation by the Holy Spirit. The Holy Spirit is the "spirit of truth" (John 14:17). It is the revelation of truth by the Holy Spirit based on the truth of Word of God that sets people free. Jesus said, *"If you hold to my teaching, you are really my disciples. Then you will know the truth, and the truth will set you free"* (John 8:31-32).

The Holy Spirit bestows special spiritual gifts that enable biblical counseling--discernment, words of knowledge and wisdom, the gifts of healing, exhortation, discerning of spirits, prophecy, and miracles. The reason why some Christian counseling fails is that some counselors do not believe these gifts are for today. These spiritual gifts were bestowed *"...to prepare God's people for works of service, so that the body of Christ may be built up until we all reach unity in the faith and in the knowledge of the Son of God and become mature, attaining to the whole measure of the fullness of Christ"* (Ephesians 4:13). Have these purposes been completely fulfilled in the Body of Christ? No. So why would these spiritual gifts be withdrawn without fulfilling God's purposes?

If you do not hear, accept, and act upon the Word of God regarding salvation, you will not be saved. If you do not hear, accept, and act upon the Word of God concerning healing, deliverance, miracles, etc., then most likely you will not experience these blessings. The Bible states that the same Spirit that raised Christ from the dead dwells in you (Romans 8:11). If that Spirit was powerful enough to raise a dead body, is it not powerful enough to meet every difficult circumstance and problem in our lives?

The Holy Spirit--with His accompanying powerful spiritual gifts--is the biblical Counselor that the whole world needs. It is because He resides within you, revealing all truth, that you--as a believer--are competent to counsel.

CHAPTER THREE

How to Deal with the "it" The Wonderful Counselor
Methods-Basis and Basics

As we look at scripture, there is no "book of counseling". The basis and basics of biblical counseling are formulated from scriptural precepts and examples, including the greatest example of all, that of our wonderful Counselor, the Lord Jesus Christ.

There are three Hebrew words translated "counsel" in scripture. Taken together, they mean to deliberate, resolve, advise, guide, determine, purpose, consult, instruct, and plan. There are five Greek verbs for the word "counsel" which, when summarized, mean to beseech, exhort, encourage, comfort, admonish, and warn. All of these are components of biblical counseling.

There are basically three approaches to counseling:

-Expert knowledge: Based on research, education, and the work of secular psychologists.

-Common or traditional knowledge: Based on experience, observation, or knowledge passed down by traditions or previous generations.

-Divine knowledge: Based on God's Word.

Although the first two may have some merit, it is divine knowledge based on God's Word that provides the basis and basics of biblical counseling. This type of counseling is rooted in what the Word of God teaches regarding acceptable behavior, positive relationships, problem-solving, and conflict resolution.

THE BASIS OF BIBLICAL COUNSELING

The principles and examples provided within the pages of God's Word provide the basis for biblical counseling. These include scriptural models of biblical counselors.

Jesus is the greatest model of a biblical counselor. As we look at Christ's ministry, we see that His goal in every encounter was to effect change that would result in abundant life. At the beginning of His ministry, Jesus declared:

The Spirit of the Lord [is] upon Me, because He has anointed Me [the Anointed one, the Messiah] to preach the good news (the Gospel) to the poor; He has sent Me to announce release to the captives and recovery of sight to the blind, to send forth as delivered those who are oppressed [who are downtrodden, bruised, crushed, and broken down by calamity], To proclaim the accepted and acceptable year of the Lord [the day when salvation and the free favors of God profusely abound.] (Luke 4:18, AMP)

The following, qualities vital to effective counseling, were evident in the ministry of Christ:

-He loved people: John 3:16.
-He confronted people when necessary: Matthew 8:26; 18:15; John 8:3-11.
-He did not condemn people: John 8:11.
-He sought to save those who were lost: Luke 19:10.
-He ministered abundant life: John 10:10.
-He destroyed the works of the devil: 1 John 3:8.
-He spoke only what God told Him to speak: John 12:49.
-He spoke with authority: Matthew 7:29.
-His ministry was empowered by prayer: Luke 5:15-16; 6:12-13.
-He had compassion: Mark 1:41; 6:34; 8:2.
-He ministered in power: Luke 5:17.
-He made people take personal responsibility for their problems: Luke 5:24; John 5.
-He dealt with root causes: In Mark 2:5 He forgave sins first, then dealt with other needs.

Volumes have been written on counseling, from both Christian and secular viewpoints, and much of it is quite complex. As we look at the ministry of Jesus, however, we see that His encounters were simple, powerful, direct, and the results were immediate. He never referred people to secular resources, nor did He tell them it would take a long time for them to receive help.

The Apostle Paul is another great example of a biblical counselor. He said, *"For you know that we dealt with each of you as a father deals with his own children, encouraging, comforting and urging you to live lives worthy of God, who calls you into his kingdom and glory"* *(1 Thessalonians 2:11-12).*

Paul's efforts were successful because, as he continues to explain, *"...when you received the word of God, which you heard from us, you accepted it not as the word of men, but as it actually is, the word of God, which is at work in you who believe" (1 Thessalonians 2:13-14).*

This is a perfect model of biblical counseling: A counselor who dispenses the Word of God as tenderly as a father deals with his own children and counselees who receive and act upon what is shared from the Word of God.

And again--if you read through Acts and the Epistles--every person to whom Paul ministered received immediate help. There were no long-term counseling sessions and no referrals to secular sources of help. Many people believe it will take a long time for them to receive help simply because someone has told them it will take a long time.

Old Testament Principles: Here are some references in the Old Testament directly related to counseling.

-The counsel of God comes through the Word: Psalm 119:24, 105.
-God is mighty in counsel: Jeremiah. 32:19; Psalm. 16:7.
-God's counsel shall stand forever: Psalm 33:11; Proverbs 19:21; Isaiah 46:10.
-Jesus Christ is called the Wonderful Counselor: Isaiah 9:6; 11:2.
-The Holy Spirit is our resident counselor: Isaiah 40:13.
-The counsel of the Lord directs the path of the believer: Psalm 73:24; 85:13;
  Proverbs 3:5,6.
-The believer is not to walk in the counsel of the ungodly: Psalm 1:1.
-It is beneficial to seek counsel from godly people: Proverbs 11:14; 15:22; 24:6.

New Testament Principles: Here are some references in the New Testament directly related to counseling.

-The Scriptures were written for our counsel: Romans 15:4; 1 Corinthians 10:11;
  2 Timothy 3:10,17.
-God's counsel is immutable--meaning it does not change: Hebrews 6:17.
-Jesus, the Counselor, prayed that the Father would send another Comforter, the Holy
  Spirit: John 14:16,26; 15:26; 16:7.
-Part of the ministry of pastors is to counsel their people: 1 Thessalonians 5:12.
-Believers are to counsel one another: Romans 15:14; Colossians 3:16.
-Children are to be counseled in the ways of the Lord: Ephesians 6:4.
-Exhortation is one of the responsibilities of the church: Romans 12:8.
-The word "admonition", meaning counsel, is used in 1 Corinthians 10:11; Ephesians.
  6:4; and Titus 3:10.
-The term "to admonish" is used in Acts 20:31; Romans 15:1-4; 1 Corinthians 4:14;
  Colossians 1:28; 3:16; 1 Thessalonians 5:12,14.

THE BASICS OF BIBLICAL COUNSELING

The following are basic premises of biblical counseling:

The counselor must be a believer. You cannot provide adequate scriptural counsel if you have not been born-again as detailed in John chapter 3. As a believer, your mind is renewed so you can understand the things of God that unbelievers cannot comprehend. You are then empowered to counsel with the ability of the mind of Christ:

The man without the Spirit does not accept the things that come from the Spirit of God, for they are foolishness to him, and he cannot understand them, because they are spiritually discerned. The spiritual man makes judgments about all things...For who has known the mind of the Lord that he may instruct him? But we have the mind of Christ. (1 Corinthians 2:14-16)

The counselee must be a believer. Unbelievers cannot understand, receive, and act upon scriptural counsel with an unregenerate mind. A personal relationship with Jesus Christ is fundamental to the biblical resolution of problems.

Biblical counsel is based on God's Word. It is not your experiences, ideas, or expertise that will help a counselee. It is not applying secular psychological models that transforms lives. It is the Word of God that effects true change:

... so is my word that goes out from my mouth: It will not return to me empty, but will accomplish what I desire and achieve the purpose for which I sent it. (Isaiah 55:11)

Biblical counseling is done by believers who base their counsel on God's Word, as opposed to counselors who--though they may be believers--base their counsel on secular philosophies. The Apostle Paul said that he had not neglected to proclaim the whole counsel of God (Acts 20:27). What was the counsel Paul gave? The entirety of God's Word.

Biblical counselors believe that the Holy Bible is the inspired Word of God and that it is the final authority regarding faith and practice:

All Scripture is given by inspiration of God, and is profitable for doctrine, for reproof, for correction, for instruction in righteousness, that the man of God may be complete, thoroughly equipped for every good work. (1 Timothy 3:16-17, NKJV)

Biblical counselors do not view the Bible as something to try to see if it works, nor do they view it as an option among others to be explored. It is the inspired Word of the one and only God. It is the answer to every need.

The Bible is profitable for:

-Doctrine--by which one can know truth, and it is the truth that sets people free.

-Reproof--by which we become aware of our sinful condition through the conviction of the Holy Spirit, without which there will be no real and lasting change.

-Correction--by which we learn how to overcome sinful habits, failures, and weaknesses, putting off the old, sinful life-style of the flesh.

-Instruction in righteousness--adapting a lifestyle which includes continuous study of God's Word, regular prayer, and involvement in a fellowship of true believers.

Secular counseling is void of this life-changing Word of God.

The counselee must agree to the authority of God's Word. The person you are counseling may be a believer, but may reject a portion of the Word of God because they don't want to act upon what it says. They may want to retain sinful emotions such as anger and unforgiveness, continue harmful habits and addictions, or refuse to sever sinful relationships

Others want to do things their own way. Good advice for them is: You got to where you are today by doing what you have done.   How has that worked for you?   If you want things to change, you must do something different!
The Bible warns that:

...the time will come when they will not endure sound doctrine; but after their own lusts shall they heap to themselves teachers, having itching ears; And they shall turn away their ears from the truth, and shall be turned unto fables. (2 Timothy 4:3-4, KJV)

Some people will not endure--receive and act upon--sound doctrine. They do not want to hear the truth. Many people seek counselors who will agree with what they want to do rather than tell them what God says they should do.

The biblical counselor can provide only limited help to those who do not agree to the authority of the Word. The Bible is quite clear that because...

...they hated knowledge, and did not choose the fear of the Lord: They would none of my counsel: they despised all my reproof. Therefore shall they eat of the fruit of their own way, and be filled with their own devices. (Proverbs 1:29-32, KJV)

Even Jesus could not minister effectively in His own home town because of unbelief (Matthew 13:58). People continue in their problems because they reject the Word of the Lord. If a person refuses the Word, they are not rejecting the counselor. They are rejecting God Himself (1 Samuel 8:7).

Biblical counseling is not done on the basis of human wisdom. We counsel on the basis of divine wisdom from God *"In whom are hid all the treasures of wisdom and knowledge"* *(Colossians 2:3, KJV).*

The Apostle Paul declared:

And my speech and my preaching was not with enticing words of man's wisdom, but in demonstration of the Spirit and of power: That your faith should not stand in the wisdom of men, but in the power of God. Howbeit we speak wisdom among them that are perfect: yet not the wisdom of this world, nor of the princes of this world, that come to naught.
(1 Corinthians 2:4-6, KJV):

This supernatural wisdom is based on the fear of the Lord: *"The fear of the Lord is the beginning of wisdom; all who follow his precepts have good understanding" (Psalm111:10).* The fear of the Lord is loving reverence for God, His person, His Word, and His actions (Malachi 1:5-6). When you fear God, you obey His Word (Ecclesiastes 12:13); walk in His ways (Deuteronomy 8:6); serve Him (Joshua 24:14); and depart from evil (Proverbs 3:7-8).

Biblical counseling does not require a certified counselor. Training in biblical counseling is advantageous, of course, but because the Counselor dwells within, certification is not necessary in order to help yourself or others. When David needed encouragement, he encouraged himself in the Lord (1 Samuel 30:1-6). As New Testament believers with the Counselor resident within us, we can do likewise.

When Daniel was burdened, he did not seek counseling, talk to his friends, or call his spiritual advisor. He prayed to God (Daniel 9). The psalmist David turned to the Word acknowledging that: *"Your testimonies also are my delight and my counselors" (Psalms 119:24, NKJV).*

This is not to discount the value of trained biblical counselors. The Bible declares: *"Where there is no counsel is, the people fall: but in the multitude of counsellors there is safety" (Proverbs 11:14, KJV).* But if you cannot find a Christian counselor who counsels biblically, you can still receive the help you need because the divine Counselor is resident within you and your answers are readily available in the inspired pages of scripture.

Biblical counsel aims for complete change. When David came to God seeking forgiveness for sin, he didn't ask for a patched up version of his old self. He prayed, "Create in me a clean heart"--the word "create" means something new (Psalm 51:10). The Bible assures:

Therefore, if any man be in Christ, he is a new creature: old things are passed away; behold, all things are become new. (2 Corinthians 5:17, KJV)

The counselor is not the one who effects change. The counselee does not change himself through self-effort. It is God that supernaturally changes a person from the inside out, creating a new creature in Christ. Not a patched-up version of the old person, but a completely new person!

Biblical counselors believe people are responsible for their actions. God is not interested in excuses for sinful behavior. He judges mankind on the basis of their response to Jesus Christ and whether or not their names are inscribed in the book of life:

And I saw the dead, small and great, stand before God; and the books were opened: and another book was opened, which is the book of life: and the dead were judged out of those things which were written in the books, according to their works. And the sea gave up the dead which were in it; and death and hell delivered up the dead which were in them: and they were judged every man according to their works. And death and hell were cast into the lake of fire. This is the second death. And whosoever was not found written in the book of life was cast into the lake of fire. (Revelation 20:12-15, KJV)

Biblical counseling deals with sin which is the root of dysfunction. Secular reasoning would suggest that we have "problems" instead of sins. Many problems, however, are actually sin issues--either the sin of the counselee or the sins of others committed against them. Biblical counseling will identify sin issues and deal with them scripturally.

The Bible says: *"The heart is deceitful above all things, and desperately wicked: who can know it?" (Jeremiah 17:9, KJV).* The solution to the sin problem is not rehabilitation, education, or legislation. It is regeneration through Jesus Christ:

All we like sheep have gone astray; we have turned everyone to his own way; and the Lord hath laid on him the iniquity of us all. (Isaiah 53:6, KJV)

Do not settle for tears of sorrow from a counselee who was caught in sin and is reaping the results. Don't accept excuses such as "that is just the way I am" or "I am this way because of my parents." Don't allow counselees to shift blame for their behavior to others. We are not *invited* to deal with sin, rather we are *commanded* to deal with it. The precepts given by God in His Word are not suggestions to consider. They are commandments that, when accepted and acted upon, have the power to change a person's life and eternal destiny.

Biblical counseling equips you to counsel others. The difficulties you experience for which you receive and act upon biblical counsel prepare you to help others:

Blessed be God, even the Father of our Lord Jesus Christ, the Father of mercies, and the God of all comfort; Who comforts us in all our tribulation, that we may be able to comfort those who are in any trouble, with the comfort with which we ourselves are comforted by God. (2 Corinthians 1:3-4, KJV)

All of the challenges you have experienced in your journey through life have prepared you to be competent to counsel. It is time to pass on to a needy world the comfort, encouragement, and help you have experienced through God and His Word. You have come into the Kingdom for such a time as this (Esther 4:14).

CHAPTER FOUR

How to deal with "it" The Root Causes

The Bible speaks of a spiritual root that bears bitterness (Deuteronomy 19:18). Jeremiah was told to "root out" sin (Jeremiah 1:10), and the prophet Malachi shows God dealing with the root of transgressions in the lives of His people (Malachi 4:1).

An important aspect of biblical counseling is dealing with the root causes of negative behaviors or situations. Dealing with root causes is aptly illustrated in the story of a man named Joash, an Old Testament king, who was facing a formidable enemy and came seeking advice from the Prophet Elisha.

Elisha made a powerful prophetic declaration and demonstration to Joash. He told him to take a bow and arrows in his hand. The king obliged, and Elisha placed his hands over those of the king. He told Joash to open the window towards the enemy nation of Syria. Then he commanded: *"'Shoot"; and he shot. And he said, "The arrow of the Lord's deliverance and the arrow of deliverance from Syria; for you must strike the Syrians at Aphek till you have destroyed them" (2 Kings 13:17, NKJV).*

Next, Elisha commanded the king to take the arrows and strike them on the ground. Joash complied, hitting the ground three times and then stopping. Elisha told him, *A You should have struck five or six times; then you would have struck Syria till you had destroyed it!" (2 Kings 13:19, NKJV).*   What Elisha was declaring prophetically was that the king should have persevered until the enemy was totally defeated. If you do not deal with the root causes of issues, then like an unquenched fire they will flare up again. Destroy the root and you will kill the fruit.

From this encounter, we learn several important strategies for dealing with root causes.

Win first in the secret chamber. What happened between Elisha and King Joash in the secret chamber determined the outcome of the battle with Syria.   It is what happens in the "secret chamber" with the Lord that determines the effectiveness of your counseling ministry as well as other areas in your spiritual life.

Use the Sword of the Spirit. Elisha told King Joash, "Take up the bow and arrows." The Apostle Paul said, "Take the sword of the Spirit." It is the Sword of the Spirit--which is God's Word--that makes your counseling effective and truly Christian.

Put your hands on the weapon. Elisha told the king to put his hands upon the bow, then Elisha laid his hands upon the king's hands. The biblical strategy is your hand upon the weapon of God=s Word and His hand on yours as you minister to the counselee.

Open the window. Israel's foe was to the east, so Elisha told the king to open the window eastward. God wants you to open up the "windows" of every area of the counselee's life to enable them to confront the failures, problems, and bondages caused by the enemy. Open the windows towards the enemy and prepare to attack every issue with the Word of God!

Shoot. Elisha told the king, "Shoot," and the king shot. The open window towards the enemy is not enough. The weapon in your hand is not sufficient. Even God's hand upon your hand will not win the battle. You must follow the command of the Lord of Hosts to "Shoot!" As you speak the prophetic, powerful, specific Word of God to the counselee, you will execute preemptive strikes against the work of the enemy in their lives. And God's Word does not return void. It accomplishes its supernatural purposes (Isaiah 55:11).

Persevere to the root of the issue. Elisha told the king to take the arrows and hit them on the ground as a symbol of his victory over Syria. The king did this, but only struck the ground three times and then stopped. Elisha told him that because he limited God by hitting the ground only three times, his military victory would be limited.   Elisha said the Lord wanted the enemy to be totally consumed. By striking the ground only three times, the king settled for partial victory.

The Lord's objective for you and the person you counsel is total victory in every area of life and ministry. You must attack the root causes of problems and battle spiritually until you have achieved 100% victory.

THE POINT OF DECISION

The New Testament records two powerful stories about people who came to a point of decision, but refused to deal with root issues in their lives. The first is that of a rich young ruler.

A certain ruler asked him, "Good teacher, what must I do to inherit eternal life?" "Why do you call me good?" Jesus answered. "No one is good--except God alone. You know the commandments: 'Do not commit adultery, do not murder, do not steal, do not give false testimony, honor your father and mother.' 'All these I have kept since I was a boy," he said. When Jesus heard this, he said to him, "You still lack one thing. Sell everything you have and give to the poor, and you will have treasure in heaven. Then come, follow me." When he heard this, he became very sad, because he was a man of great wealth. (Luke 18:18-23)

This young man was a good, moral, law-abiding person. He had kept many commandments of the Word of God faithfully, but he had a root issue in his life that needed correction. He valued money more than His commitment to the Lord. This was evident when Jesus told him to sell what he had and come and follow Him. Sadly, the young man rejected Christ's counsel, went his own way, and missed his divine destiny.

The second story is that of a multitude of disciples who were following Jesus. They were excited about the miracles they were witnessing and the anointed teaching they were receiving. But when the Lord shared truths that they did not want to accept, many of them turned back and no longer followed Him (John 6:66). The root of the problem was that they rejected the Word of the Lord and this resulted in them turning back to the old life.

In every counseling situation, there is a root cause of problems that must be exposed on the basis of the scriptures. It is at that point that the counselee will either accept or refuse God's Word. Sadly, many are like the rich young ruler and these followers of Jesus. They refuse the Word, go away sorrowing, and return to their old life.

Do not perceive responses like this as personal rejection or failure in your ministry of counseling. The Bible states: *"Therefore, he who rejects this instruction does not reject man but God, who gives you his Holy Spirit" (1 Thessalonians 4:8).*

WHAT IS THE ROOT CAUSE?

It is vital that you persevere to discover the root cause of every problem. For example, the root cause is not drug addiction, it is what is fueling the drug addiction. The root cause is not immorality, it is the lust resulting in the immoral behavior.

The Bible commands us to diligently seek and destroy the roots of sinful behavior:

Looking diligently lest any man fail of the grace of God; lest any root of bitterness springing up trouble you, and thereby many be defiled. (Hebrews 12:15)

If the root causes of problems are not dealt with, then problems will only intensify. When Israel invaded the promised land, God told them not to allow any of the enemy to remain. But the Bible records that Joshua spared giants in three cities: Gaza, Ashdod, and Gath (Joshua 11:21-22). Later, the Bible relates that Samson got in trouble in Gaza (Joshua 16); the ark of God=s glory was lost in Ashdod (1 Samuel 4-5); and Goliath paralyzed the troops of Israel in Gath (1 Samuel 17). None of these tragedies would have occurred, had not the giants been left in the land. Israel left a root, and it bore fruit. Giants beget giants in both the natural and spiritual worlds. Eliminate the spiritual giants of sin and they will no longer reproduce.

Deal with the root causes, and the surface manifestations will cease. As in the natural world, so it is in the spiritual: Cut the root and you will kill the fruit of the root.

CHAPTER FIVE

How to deal the "it" The Spiritually Dead

People come for counseling because they have experienced some sort of death. It may be the actual death of a loved one, the loss of a meaningful relationship, or lost dreams. It may be the death of hope that things can change in their lives, or they may be experiencing the terrors of the spiritual death of sin.

The Bible provides an excellent example that is applicable to counseling, in that it provides strategies for raising the spiritually dead to new life. The story is found in 2 Kings 4 where the Prophet Elisha raises a young boy from the dead.

Elisha was a frequent guest in a special room prepared by a Shunammite woman and her husband. Despite the fact that this woman did not have a child and her husband was elderly and beyond child-producing years, Elisha prophesied that she would conceive and bear a son (2 Kings 4:16).

Just as Elisha declared, the woman gave birth to a son. Years passed, and then one day when the boy was out in the field with his father, he became sick and died. The Shunammite woman took her dead son to Elisha's room and laid him on the prophet=s bed. She quickly saddled a donkey and set out with her servant to go to Elisha at Mt. Carmel. Imagine the thoughts that flooded her mind: AWhy had this terrible thing happened? Why had God allowed the son He had given her to die?@ Very often, similar questions are asked by hurting people: "Why did God allow this to happen to me?"

Although she knew her boy=s lifeless body lay upon the prophet's bed, this woman did not focus on her tragic circumstances. She believed that if she could just get to Elisha, the prophet of God would be able to help her. She hurriedly prepared for her journey and told her husband, *AYIt is well@,* in answer to his questions regarding her journey (2 Kings 4:23).

When Elisha saw the woman coming at a distance, he sent his servant Gehazi to meet her and ask if everything was alright. The woman told the servant that all was well, but when she saw Elisha she ran to him and fell at his feet. Gehazi tried to push her away, but Elisha told him to leave her alone.

ADid I ask you for a son? Didn=t I tell you, 'do not deceive me'@, the woman cried out in anguish as she shared her tragedy with Elisha (2 Kings 4:28). Elisha immediately commanded Gehazi to take his staff in his hand and run to the Shunammite=s house to minister to the boy, but the Shunammite woman refused to settle for that. She was desperate! She was determined to persevere until Elisha agreed to go with her. He was the prophet of God and she wanted him to cry out to God for the life of her boy (2 Kings 4:30). When Elisha saw her determination, he finally agreed to go with her.

THE POWER OF PERSEVERANCE

This Shunammite woman was determined to persevere in behalf of her son regardless of the seemingly impossible circumstances. There may be tremendous obstacles standing in your way or the way of your counselee, barriers blocking you from receiving help. You must identify and eliminate these through the power of God.

Whatever need you or a counselee may face--whether it be a personal issue, an emotional problem, a financial need, or a physical challenge--you must focus on the faithfulness of God instead of the circumstances. Your faith must not be limited by the need, your own limited abilities, or by what you see with your natural eyes. You must persevere in the Spirit to receive a miracle.

Jesus taught that we should believe we have received what we have asked for when we pray. He said, *AY Therefore I tell you, whatever you ask for in prayer, believe that you have received it, and it will be yours@ (Mark 11:24).* By eyes of faith, look beyond the natural circumstances into the supernatural realm where all things are possible with God--including your own deliverance and that of those you are counseling.

The servant, Gehazi, arrived ahead of Elisha and the mother, entered the room where the lifeless body lay on the bed, and placed Elisha=s staff on the boy=s face. Nothing happened. Gehazi went to meet Elisha and told him that the boy had not awakened (2 Kings 4:31). This did not discourage Elisha, however. He did not reverse his direction to return to Mount Carmel. Elisha knew God=s power was stronger than death--and that same power is greater than any need you or your counselee may be facing.

When Elisha reached the house, he went into his room and shut the door. Alone in that room, facing the boy=s corpse, he began to cry out to God with great fervency. Then Elisha spread himself over the boy=s body and the life of God began to flow through him into the boy. The child's body grew warm, but was still lifeless. Elisha got up and walked back and forth in the room.

A second time Elisha stretched himself on the boy=s lifeless body and suddenly--the power of God broke the chains of death. The life of God entered the boy, raised him from the dead, and the child sneezed seven times as the breath of life entered into him. Elisha immediately sent for the Shunammite woman and presented her son to her alive and well.

New life. That is the purpose of biblical counseling.

The Bible says the soul that sins will die, that the wages of sin is death, and that sinners are dead in their transgressions. People coming to you for help are dead in sin, have buried dreams, lost hope, and dying relationships. The following spiritual applications, drawn from this account of Elisha, may be applied as you provide counsel to raise the spiritually dead.

Have faith. The mother did not just accept the child's death. The normal response would be to weep, call professional mourners, and prepare the body for burial. Instead, she laid him on Elisha=s bed, shut the door, and went to get the prophet. Taking the dead child to the prophet's chamber was an act of faith in itself, as she most likely recalled the well-known miracle previously done by the Prophet Elijah (1 Kings 17:17-24). This woman did not wait for the prophet to take him into the room. She took him there, expecting a miracle. God has raised spiritually dead men from the beginning of time. Your privilege, as a biblical counselor, is to take unsaved and troubled people--just as they are--to the place of a miracle.

Note this woman=s faith when she responded to her husband's questions, *"It shall be well"* (verses 23-24). When you begin to act by faith, your faith multiplies. By the time she neared the prophet's dwelling place, her faith had increased (verse 26). When Elisha sent Gehazi to question her, she no longer said, A*It shall be well."* She said, *"It is well."* It is not only important for you, as a counselor to have faith, but you must instill faith in the counselee that things can change. Prepare them to receive a miracle!

Make haste. Note in 2 Kings 4:22 that the woman said, "That I may run." You must make haste to raise the dead because souls are perishingBright now, today, this very hour. Relationships are shattering. Homes are breaking up. Bondages are engulfing people in a death-like grip. Someone is at the point of suicide. There is no time for years of extended counseling. The miracle is needed now!

Break with tradition. In verse 23, the woman=s husband questioned, "Why are you going?" It was not a traditional time to go to the prophet such as on the new moon or the Sabbath. To counsel biblically, you will have to break with tradition. People may tell you, "This is not the way we do things." They may claim your methods are faulty and unscientific. But if your counsel is based on God's Word, it will work! Guaranteed success!

Show compassion. The dead will never be raised by "Gehazis" who have no compassion (verses 25-27). When this woman came in search of life, Gehazi wanted to send her away--which is what many church leaders are doing today--referring people with needs to others so they do not have to deal with their problems. But the Prophet of God did not send her away. He showed concern and asked, "Is it well with you and your husband and the child?"

CHAPTER SIX

How to deal with "it" Prayer in Biblical Counseling

Prayer is not only the spiritual life blood for all believers, it is vital in biblical counseling. Prayer, along with the Word of God and the ministry of the Holy Spirit, is what makes counseling truly Christian.

Before the session.   The Bible declares that ", *our struggle is not against flesh and blood, but...against the spiritual forces of evil in the heavenly realms" (Ephesians 6:12).* Spiritual warfare will be waged in every counseling session because you are battling for the spiritual, mental, emotional, and physical well-being of counselees.

Ask the Holy Spirit to release the spirit of wisdom and understanding in preparation for the counseling session. Ask God to fight the battle for you. The real battle of spiritual warfare in counseling is won in private in prayer before the session ever begins. Intercede for the person you are to counsel. *"Intercession may be defined as holy, believing, persevering prayer whereby someone pleads with God on behalf of another or others who desperately need God's intervention."*

Opening the session. Pray with and for the counselee when you start the counseling session. This sets the focus, acknowledging that both the counselor and the counselee are looking to God for guidance.

During the session. Prayer can be incorporated during the session as specific problems are discussed. Deal with issues immediately in prayer. This gets the counselee's focus back on God instead of his problems.

Allow the Holy Spirit to speak *through you* in prayer and speak *to you* about the issues you are addressing.   He is the resident Counselor and scriptures confirm that...

...the Spirit also helps in our weaknesses. For we do not know what we should pray for as we ought, but the Spirit Himself makes intercession for us with groanings which cannot be uttered. Now He who searches the hearts knows what the mind of the Spirit is, because He makes intercession for the saints according to the will of God.
(Romans 8:26-27, NKJV)

It is the will of God that is being sought in counseling, and the Holy Spirit accurately prays that will into being. So allow the Holy Spirit to intercede through you as you counsel.

Concluding the session. The session should always end with prayer by both the counselor and the counselee. The counselor should pray for the counselee and incorporate summary statements regarding issues discussed into his prayer. Inviting the counselee to pray concerning their problems will help them learn to communicate with God for themselves. If a person is uncomfortable with praying audibly, dedicate a few minutes of quiet time before ending the session so the counselee can pray silently about the issues that have been discussed.

CHAPTER SEVEN

How to deal with "it" Basics Counseling Strategies

The strategies of a biblical counselor are based on the Word of God. Here are some basics to guide your counseling ministry.

Start every session with prayer. This establishes that the interchange is not just to be a discussion of various options or opinions on an issue. Express your reliance upon the power of God, and expect that power to be manifested as you counsel. Ask the Holy Spirit for guidance, because what you see or hear on the surface may not be the real problem. Ask for divine revelation of the true issues that need to be addressed.

Ask questions. Jesus did this--not because He didn't know the answer--but to help a person seeking help to clarify their need.

Jesus stopped and ordered the man to be brought to him. When he came near, Jesus asked him, "What do you want me to do for you?" "Lord, I want to see," he replied. Jesus said to him, "Receive your sight; your faith has healed you." Immediately he received his sight and followed Jesus, praising God. When all the people saw it, they also praised God. (Luke 18:40-43)

If the counselee tends to ramble, questions will help them refocus on the subject of concern. Ask the person to state a problem clearly: "My problem is....." Restate the problem in a manner that you and the counselee can agree on, such as: "As I understand it, you are saying that your problem is....."

Stop, look, and listen. Jesus modeled this when He took time to stop and listen to the cries of desperate people, and to look beyond the surface appearances to identify their true needs. Sometimes, all that someone needs is a person to listen to them, rather than to dispense advice (Job 31:35). Do not judge, criticize, or condemn. Just listen. You do not have to fill a void of silence if one occurs. Allow times of silence in order for the counselee to think and for the Holy Spirit to provide direction. Don't interrupt, rather hear them out (Proverbs 18:13). Pay attention to how they express the facts and their feelings. Sometimes a counselee will actually talk themselves into their own biblical solution!

Deal with root causes. As you have learned in this introductory section, it is vital that root causes be identified and dealt with. For example, a man may appear to be concerned about his marriage, but his appearance may indicate that he has been drinking heavily. His root problem may not be his marriage, but rather his addiction to alcohol.

Dealing with the root problem of sin is a priority. When a bedridden man was brought to Jesus for healing, the Lord perceived that his sin was the priority rather than his physical condition:

A few days later, when Jesus again entered Capernaum, the people heard that he had come home. So many gathered that there was no room left, not even outside the door, and he preached the word to them. Some men came, bringing to him a paralytic, carried by four of them. Since they could not get him to Jesus because of the crowd, they made an opening in the roof above Jesus and, after digging through it, lowered the mat the paralyzed man was lying on. When Jesus saw their faith, he said to the paralytic, "Son, your sins are forgiven." (Mark 2:1-5)

Jesus dealt with the sin problem first, then He healed the paralytic man.

When Jesus asked the crippled man at the pool of Bethesda if he wanted to be healed, his answer was not a resounding "Yes!" Instead he said, *"Sir," the invalid replied, "I have no one to help me into the pool when the water is stirred. While I am trying to get in, someone else goes down ahead of me" (John 5:7)*. This man was so busy complaining and feeling sorry for himself that he didn't realize who was standing right there before him. He was looking for a person to help him, rather than looking to God. After Jesus healed this lame man, He told him, *"... See, you are well again. Stop sinning or something worse may happen to you" (John 5:14)*. Not all infirmity is caused by personal sin (John 9:3), but apparently this man's disability was a result of his sin.

Identify the problems. Through prayer, attentive listening, and the guidance of the Holy Spirit clarify the issues troubling the counselee.

Ask what the person has done to try to solve their problem. If the methods are unscriptural, point out that there is no need to try these methods again since they did not work. Direct them towards biblical solutions. If they have tried biblical solutions and given up, emphasize the importance of perseverance in securing spiritual victories (Matthew 15:22-28). Do not criticize other counselors, pastors, chaplains, ministries or agencies. Concentrate on responding positively rather than minimizing what others have tried to do or failed to do for them.

Provide counsel based on God's Word. There are two main approaches to counseling, directive and non-directive:

> **Directive counseling:** The counselor tells the person what to do. The counselor assumes more of a dominant role, using the Word of God as the source of authority. Confrontation, challenge, and admonition characterize this approach.

> **Non-directive counseling:** The counselor guides the counselee in arriving at solutions based on the Word of God. The counselor is more of a facilitator than an initiator. Encouragement, support, and empathy characterize this approach.

So which approach is best? It is not an either/or question. Each method has limitations, but both can be used effectively with the guidance of the Holy Spirit.

The Apostle Paul provides a good model of this. In some cases he aggressively confronted and commanded people to conform to God's Word. In others, he guided them as a father does a child to arrive at the proper solution (1 Thessalonians 2:7-12).

Jesus was directive with those who were hard-hearted and rebellious--people like the Pharisees and Sadducees (Matthew 15:1-20). With others, He was non-directive, using questions to draw them out and allowing them see what was in their hearts (John 4:1-26).

Use the Biblical Counseling Database. Use this database to clarify what God's Word says about specific problems. For example, if their battle is with anger, use the "Anger" topic in the database. If they are having an affair, use the topic of "Adultery". Through sharing specific insights from the *Biblical Counseling Database*, a natural flow of conversation will ensue during which you can explain how the scriptures can be effectively applied to their problems. Sharing from your own personal experience, if applicable, may be helpful. But remember: It is not your experiences that will provide solutions to problems--it is God's Word.

You do not have to provide an immediate answer for every issue raised by the counselee. You may have to tell a person that you need to research a certain problem more thoroughly in the Word of God. It is better to say nothing, than to say the wrong thing. Constantly check what you are advising with the *Biblical Counseling Database* and your ultimate counseling guide, the Word of God.

Develop a plan of action. Once a problem has been discussed and scriptural counsel given, a plan of action should be developed on the basis of the Word of God. Do not make this complex. What is a simple first step which can be taken towards the solution to their problem? For example: Do they need to ask forgiveness of someone? Encourage them to do so. Do they need to make restitution?   Formulate a plan.

No two problems are exactly alike, so no two plans of action will be identical. All action steps, however, should be based upon God's Word. By the end of a counseling session there should be a plan--even if it is a very small step--that can be made to institute change. To be most effective, the counselor should follow-up on the plan, holding the counselee accountable to take the steps agreed upon in a timely manner.

Conclude the session in prayer. Pray for the counselee. Be specific in your prayer. If they need deliverance, pray a prayer of deliverance. If they need forgiveness for sin, lead them in a prayer regarding this. If they need to forgive others, pray a pray of relinquishment and forgiveness. Have the counselee pray audibly or silently, whichever they feel most comfortable doing.

Provide the counselee with feedback from the session. Use this database to provide the counselee with feedback on the topic or topics with which you dealt in counseling. This will enable them to study further on biblical principles relating to their problems. Add to the feedback the action steps which you have agreed upon and a realistic timeline in which these might be completed. Print a hardcopy of the document or email it to the counselee.

CONFIDENTIALITY

Whether you are a professional biblical counselor, chaplain, minister, or simply a believer helping others, you must keep counseling sessions confidential.

In the United States, a certified doctor, lawyer, counselor, and minister are protected by law from being forced to reveal confidential information shared by a client. This may be true in other nations as well. Check the confidentiality laws of your nation.

The following are exceptions to confidentiality--legal or moral obligations where you should break the rule of confidentiality:

-Child abuse or molestation: Report this to the proper authorities immediately.

-Suicide in progress: If you receive a telephone call of a suicide in progress, keep the caller on the line and talking with you while you have someone else dial emergency services to dispatch assistance. Use Appendix One of this database for guidelines in handling this type of counseling call.

-Violence in progress: If you receive a counseling call where violence is in progress, keep the caller on the line and have someone else call emergency services to dispatch assistance.

CHAPTER EIGHT

How to seal with "it" Goals of Biblical Counseling

The immediate goals of counseling are:

-To guide the counselee in identifying and stating his problem.
-To provide scriptural counsel for dealing with the problem.
-To help the counselee find salvation, forgiveness, healing, deliverance, comfort, and answers to problems through application of scriptural principles.
-To promote biblical change that will transform lives.

With this in mind, the following spiritual foundations should be emphasized: Salvation, water baptism, baptism in the Holy Spirit, sanctified living, spiritual warfare, and developing the Fruit of the Spirit. The Word of God, prayer, and membership in a Bible-believing church are also essential.

As a biblical counselor, you are not aiming for self-improvement or rehabilitation. You don't want a patched-up version of the old person. Rather, your goal is total transformation through Jesus Christ:

Therefore, if anyone is in Christ, he is a new creation; the old has gone, the new has come! All this is from God, who reconciled us to himself through Christ and gave us the ministry of reconciliation: that God was reconciling the world to himself in Christ, not counting men's sins against them. And he has committed to us the message of reconciliation. We are therefore Christ's ambassadors, as though God were making his appeal through us. We implore you on Christ's behalf: Be reconciled to God.
(2 Corinthians 5:17-21)

As a biblical counselor, you are to lead people to experience transformation that results in new life, reconciling them to God through Jesus Christ. You are Christ's ambassador, and He is making His appeal through you to a lost and needy world.

The end results of biblical counseling can be summed up in three phrases. The counselee must eventually:

-Admit it: Admit that what they are doing is wrong or that what was done to them was wrong.

-Quit it: If what they are doing is sinful, they need to ask forgiveness from God and quit doing wrong. If what was done to them by others was wrong, they need to quit nursing it and rehearsing it, and they must forgive their offender.

-Forget it: When God forgives, He forgets. The counselee must do likewise--forget the wrongs they have done and those they have suffered from the sinful actions of others.

The bottom line is, on the basis of God's Word: Admit it, quit it, forget it.

Before concluding counseling, be sure the counselee is involved in a local church. If not, refer them to a church where further Christian growth, fellowship, and spiritual counsel can continue.

At some point in biblical counseling, a counselee must either accept or reject what God has to say regarding their problems. When the Word of God is rejected, no further progress can be made in terms of biblical counseling until the counselee agrees to what God says about his issues. Jesus asked His disciples, *"Why do you call me 'Lord, Lord' and do not do what I say?" (Luke 6:46).* A person cannot truly acknowledge Jesus as Lord unless they totally commit to doing His will.

The Old Testament leper, Naaman, initially rebelled against the Word of the Lord from the Prophet Elisha. Eventually, however, Naaman obeyed that Word and he received total restoration. No more leprosy. New skin. A new life! As a result, Naaman acknowledged that there was no other God in the world other than the one who had just made him whole (2 Kings 5:15). That is the testimony of those who receive and act upon the Word of God you deliver in biblical counseling.

DO NOT SEND THEM AWAY

When a weary, hungry, weak crowd gathered around the disciples, these men asked Jesus to send the multitude away:

Late in the afternoon the Twelve came to him and said, "Send the crowd away so they can go to the surrounding villages and countryside and find food and lodging, because we are in a remote place here." (Luke 9:12)

But Jesus replied, *"You give them something to eat" (Luke 9:13).*

There are multitudes of spiritually hungry people who are too weak to go any further down the road of life. Will you send them away, or will you give them something to eat?

Like the disciples, you may feel inadequate for the task--they only had five loaves of bread and two fish. But these weren't just any loaves of bread and fish. These elements were supernaturally multiplied because of the blessing upon them. You hold in your hands the Holy Scriptures--the supernaturally infused nourishment that is blessed by God and desperately needed by a spiritually hungry world.

God's cry through the Prophet Hosea was *"I would have healed them..."*--but His counsel was rejected (Hosea 7). The balm of Gilead is only effective when applied (Jeremiah 8:22).

As a biblical counselor, your purpose is to apply the spiritual balm of God's Word and share the bread of life with hurting men and women.

God's stated purpose is that... "*...My word be that goes forth from My mouth; It shall not return to Me void, but it shall accomplish what I please, and it shall prosper in the thing for which I sent it" (Isaiah 55:11, NKJV).*

CHAPTER NINE

How to deal with "it" Establishing a Phone Counseling Ministry

-Set aside a private room for telephone counseling.

-Establish one or more dedicated phone lines for receiving calls.

-Phones should have hands-free headsets so counselors can write and/or use a computer terminal.

-Appoint a telephone counseling ministry coordinator who will recruit, train, and schedule counselors.

-Recruiting counselors.
    -Recruits must be born-again, as this is biblical counseling.
    -Recruits should be able to read and write in order to use the database effectively.
    -Recruits should be seasoned believers who are well-versed in the Word of God.
    -Recruits should be faithful men and women who follow-through on their commitments.
    -Recruits should express a passion for this type of ministry.

-Establish prayer support. Not everyone can or should be a telephone counselor, but you can involve everyone in praying for the ministry.

-Training counselors:
    -Use the introductory chapters of this manual.
    -Train recruits in how to use the database.
    -Advise that if a caller is using obscene, vulgar, or abusive language, they should terminate the call.
    -Warn recruits to never give medical advice, i.e., advising a caller to stop taking medication.
    -Warn recruits that they should never give legal advice.

-Establish a call schedule. Set regular hours for the telephone counseling ministry. Weekday evenings are generally the most active time for receiving calls, so fill these time slots first. Weekends are usually the least active.

-Advertise the telephone counseling ministry in the church bulletin, local newspapers, flyers, churches, local media, and small business-sized cards.

CHAPTER TEN

How to deal with "it" Establishing a Life Coaching Ministry

Life coaches are believers who are not necessarily certified as professional counselors, but who have a desire to help others find biblical guidance for their problems. Many churches have opted to train lay-counselors so that the responsibility for the counseling ministry does not rest solely upon the senior pastor. Here are some steps to establish a lay-counseling ministry.

-Set aside a private room for counseling.

-Appoint a life coach ministry coordinator who will recruit, train, and schedule coaches.

-Recruiting coaches.
    -Recruits must be born-again, as this is biblical counseling.
    -Recruits should be able to read and write in order to use the database effectively.
    -Recruits should be seasoned believers who are well-versed in the Word of God.
    -Recruits should be faithful men and women who follow-through on their commitments.
    -Recruits should express a passion for this type of ministry.

-Establish prayer support. Not everyone can or should be a counselor, but you can involve everyone in praying for the ministry.

-Training counselors:
    -Use the introductory chapters of this manual.
    -Train recruits in how to use the database.
    -Advise that if a counselee uses obscene, vulgar, or abusive language, they should terminate the counseling session.
    -Warn recruits to never give medical advice, i.e., advising a person to stop taking medication.
    -Warn recruits that they should never give legal advice.

-Establish a counseling schedule, days and hours the center will be open and staffed.

-Advertise the Life Coaching ministry in the church bulletin, local newspapers, flyers, churches, local media, and through small business-sized cards.

CHAPTER ELEVEN
How to deal with "it" Put off and Put on

Several passages in the Bible command believers to put off certain behaviors and put on others, to "clothe themselves", and to "let" or allow certain qualities to be manifested in their lives. Acting upon these passages will enable you to overcome practically every challenge you will face in your counseling as well as in your own life.

Therefore **do not let sin reign** in your mortal body so that you obey its evil desires. **Do not offer the parts of your body to sin**, as instruments of wickedness, but rather **offer yourselves to God**, as those who have been brought from death to life; and **offer the parts of your body** to him as instruments of righteousness. For sin shall not be your master, because you are not under law, but under grace. (Romans 6:12-14)

Let no debt remain outstanding, except the continuing debt to love one another, for he who loves his fellowman has fulfilled the law. The commandments, "Do not commit adultery," "Do not murder," "Do not steal," "Do not covet," and whatever other commandment there may be, are summed up in this one rule: "**Love your neighbor as yourself.**" Love does no harm to its neighbor. Therefore love is the fulfillment of the law. (Romans 13:8-10)

The night is nearly over; the day is almost here. So **let us put** aside the deeds of darkness and **put on** the armor of light. **Let us behave decently**, as in the daytime, not in orgies and drunkenness, not in sexual immorality and debauchery, not in dissension and jealousy. Rather, **clothe yourselves** with the Lord Jesus Christ, and **do not think about** how to gratify the desires of the sinful nature. (Romans 13:12-14)

Therefore **let us stop passing judgment on one another**. Instead, make up your mind not to put any stumbling block or obstacle in your brother's way. (Romans 14:13)

Let us therefore make every effort to do what leads to peace and to mutual edification. (Romans 14:19)

Therefore, as it is written: **"Let him who boasts boast in the Lord."** (1 Corinthians 1:31)

When I was a child, I talked like a child, I thought like a child, I reasoned like a child. When I became a man, I **put childish ways behind me**. (1 Corinthians 13:11)

Do everything in love. (1 Corinthians 16:14)

Since we have these promises, dear friends, **let us purify ourselves from everything that contaminates** body and spirit, perfecting holiness out of reverence for God. (2 Corinthians 7:1)

For the perishable must clothe itself with the imperishable, and the mortal with immortality. When the perishable has been clothed with the imperishable, and the mortal with immortality, then the saying that is written will come true: "Death has been swallowed up in victory." "Where, O death, is your victory? Where, O death, is your sting?"   The sting of death is sin, and the power of sin is the law. But thanks be to God! He gives us the victory through our Lord Jesus Christ. Therefore, my dear brothers, **stand firm. Let nothing move you.** Always give yourselves fully to the work of the Lord, because you know that your labor in the Lord is not in vain. (1 Corinthians 15:53-58)

Put off the works of the flesh: The acts of the sinful nature are obvious: sexual immorality, impurity and debauchery; idolatry and witchcraft; hatred, discord, jealousy, fits of rage, selfish ambition, dissensions, factions and envy; drunkenness, orgies, and the like. I warn you, as I did before, that those who live like this will not inherit the kingdom of God. (Galatians 5:19-21)

Put on the fruit of the Spirit: But the fruit of the Spirit is love, joy, peace, patience, kindness, goodness, faithfulness, gentleness and self-control. Against such things there is no law. Those who belong to Christ Jesus have crucified the sinful nature with its passions and desires. Since we live by the Spirit, let us keep in step with the Spirit. Let us not become conceited, provoking and envying each other. (Galatians 5:22-26)

Let us not become weary in doing good, for at the proper time we will reap a harvest if we do not give up. (Galatians 6:9)

You were taught, with regard to your former way of life, **to put off your old self**, which is being corrupted by its deceitful desires; to be made new in the attitude of your minds; and **to put on the new self**, created to be like God in true righteousness and holiness. Therefore each of you must **put off** falsehood and speak truthfully to his neighbor, for we are all members of one body. In your anger do not sin: **Do not let** the sun go down while you are still angry, and **do not give the devil a foothold**. He who has been stealing must steal no longer, but must work, doing something useful with his own hands, that he may have something to share with those in need. **Do not let** any unwholesome talk come out of your mouths, but only what is helpful for building others up according to their needs, that it may benefit those who listen. And **do not grieve the Holy Spirit of God**, with whom you were sealed for the day of redemption. **Get rid of** all bitterness, rage and anger, brawling and slander, along with every form of malice. Be kind and compassionate to one another, forgiving each other, just as in Christ God forgave you. (Ephesians 4:22-32)

Let no one deceive you with empty words, for because of such things God's wrath comes on those who are disobedient. Therefore do not be partners with them. (Ephesians 5:6-7)

Whatever happens, **conduct yourselves in a manner worthy** of the gospel of Christ. (Philippians 1:27)

Rejoice in the Lord always. I will say it again: Rejoice! **Let your gentleness be evident to all.** The Lord is near. **Do not be anxious about anything**, but in everything, by prayer and petition, with thanksgiving, present your requests to God. And the peace of God, which transcends all understanding, will guard your hearts and your minds in Christ Jesus. (Philippians 4:4-7)

You used to walk in these ways, in the life you once lived. But now you must **rid yourselves** of all such things as these: anger, rage, malice, slander, and filthy language from your lips. **Do not** lie to each other, since you have **taken off your old self with its practices and have put on the new self**, which is being renewed in knowledge in the image of its Creator. Here there is no Greek or Jew, circumcised or uncircumcised, barbarian, Scythian, slave or free, but Christ is all, and is in all. Therefore, as God's chosen people, holy and dearly loved, **clothe yourselves** with compassion, kindness, humility, gentleness and patience. **Bear with each other** and forgive whatever grievances you may have against one another. **Forgive as the Lord forgave you**. And over all these virtues **put on** love, which binds them all together in perfect unity. **Let the peace of Christ rule in your hearts,** since as members of one body you were called to peace. **And be thankful. Let the word of Christ dwell in you richly** as you teach and admonish one another with all wisdom, and as you sing psalms, hymns and spiritual songs with gratitude in your hearts to God. And **whatever you do**, whether in word or deed, do it all in the name of the Lord Jesus, giving thanks to God the Father through him. (Colossians 3:7-17)

So then, **let us not be like others**, who are asleep, but let us be alert and self-controlled. For those who sleep, sleep at night, and those who get drunk, get drunk at night. But since we belong to the day, **let u**s be self-controlled, putting on faith and love as a breastplate, and the hope of salvation as a helmet. (1 Thessalonians 5:6-8)

Don't let anyone look down on you because you are young, but set an example for the believers in speech, in life, in love, in faith and in purity. (1 Timothy 4:12)

Therefore, since we have a great high priest who has gone through the heavens, Jesus the Son of God, **let us hold firmly to the faith we profess**. (Hebrews 4:14)

Let us then approach the throne of grace with confidence, so that we may receive mercy and find grace to help us in our time of need. (Hebrews 4:16)

Therefore, **let us leave** the elementary teachings about Christ and go on to maturity, (Hebrews 6:1)

Let us hold unswervingly to the hope we profess, for he who promised is faithful. And let us consider how we may spur one another on toward love and good deeds. **Let us not give up meeting together**, as some are in the habit of doing, but **let us encourage one another--**and all the more as you see the Day approaching. (Hebrews 10:23-25)

Therefore, since we are surrounded by such a great cloud of witnesses, **let us throw off everything that hinders and the sin that so easily entangles, and let us run with perseverance the race marked out for us. Let us fix our eyes on Jesus**, the author and perfecter of our faith, who for the joy set before him endured the cross, scorning its shame, and sat down at the right hand of the throne of God. Consider him who endured such opposition from sinful men, so that you will not grow weary and lose heart. (Hebrews 12:1-3)

Keep your lives free from the love of money and be content with what you have... (Hebrews 13: 5)

Who is wise and understanding among you? **Let him show it by his good life**, by deeds done in the humility that comes from wisdom. (James 3:13)

...All of you, **clothe yourselves** with humility toward one another, because, "God opposes the proud but gives grace to the humble."   Humble yourselves, therefore, under God's mighty hand, that he may lift you up in due time. (1 Peter 5:5-6)

Dear children, **let us not love with words or tongue** but with actions and in truth. (1 John 3:18)

Dear friends, **let us love one another**, for love comes from God. Everyone who loves has been born of God and knows God (1 John 4:7)

Finally, be strong in the Lord and in his mighty power. **Put on the full armor of God** so that you can take your stand against the devil's schemes. For our struggle is not against flesh and blood, but against the rulers, against the authorities, against the powers of this dark world and against the spiritual forces of evil in the heavenly realms. **Therefore put on the full armor of God, so that when the day of evil comes, you may be able to stand your ground, and after you have done everything, to stand**. Stand firm then, with the belt of truth buckled around your waist, with the breastplate of righteousness in place, and with your feet fitted with the readiness that comes from the gospel of peace. In addition to all this, **take up** the shield of faith, with which you can extinguish all the flaming arrows of the evil one. **Take** the helmet of salvation and the sword of the Spirit, which is the word of God. And **pray** in the Spirit on all occasions with all kinds of prayers and requests. With this in mind, **be alert** and always keep on praying for all the saints. (Ephesians 6:10-18)

CHAPTER TWELVE

How to deal with "it" Selecting A Biblical Counselor

-Pray that God will guide you to the right counselor.

-Select a biblical counselor from your home church if one is available.

-If your church does not have a biblical counselor, ask your pastor for a referral to a biblical counseling ministry in your community.

-Ask a fellow-believer for a recommendation to a biblical counselor who has helped them.

-Here are some key questions to ask a prospective counselor:
    -Are you a believer? When did you accept Christ as your Savior?
    -How does your faith affect your counseling?
    -Upon what do you base your counseling?
    -How do you incorporate prayer into your counseling?
    -How long have you been engaged in a counseling ministry?
    -Do you charge for counseling and if so, what is the fee?

-Remember that just because someone is a Christian does not mean he/she is a biblical counselor. Some Christian counselors base their counsel on secular psychology. Biblical counselors base their counsel on God's Word, not secular psychology.

-Be sure your counselor is a born-again believer.

-Be sure your counselor incorporates prayer and the Word of God into counseling.

-Counseling is an interactive process, meaning that open and honest dialogue must occur between a counselor and a counselee. If you cannot establish such dialogue, you might need to find a different counselor.

-Do not remain with a counselor who discredits God, discounts His Word, or criticizes the church and its leadership.

-Do not remain with a counselor whose lifestyle does not line up with the Word of God.

-Do not remain with a counselor who is manipulative or controlling.

CONCLUSION

How to Get Rid of "it" though Personal Deliverance

When you understand self-deliverance, you will keep yourself from being bond; you will keep yourself healthy, physically and spiritually and be free from spiritual pollution. Every day, you will enjoy divine health and will not be spending your money on drugs and hospital bills.

Sometimes, there may not be a minister who is anointed and knowledgeable about deliverance to help you. Sometimes, you can be heavily attacked and the next service is about four days away. What do you do? You should never allow evil spirits to reside in your life. If you lack adequate time to do a self-deliverance in the mornings, after your quiet time, then, when you're having your bath, you could do it.

Whatever the causes of our spiritual afflictions, there are several proven steps we may try to help ourselves find freedom and healing. If these steps do not resolve your situation, then perhaps it is time to ask for help:

Step 1 — Conversion

Deliverance from any level of bondage, or harassment (collectively called, "spiritual afflictions") cannot be achieved without personal conversion. Deliverance from milder forms of spiritual affliction may often be achieved by the various acts of personal conversion—Acts of Contrition, Faith, Hope, Charity, and Consecration. "Prayer Acts" and other prayers, with fasting, and various devotions are often effective to drive evil spirits away:

So humble yourselves before God. Resist the Devil, and he will flee from you. Draw close to God, and God will draw close to you. — (James 4:7,8)

The first step, therefore, is make up your mind to live the Christ-life; or if already doing so, to persevere in living the Christ-life. This internal conversion, which is a conscious decision and determination to follow Christ and all of His teachings, precedes all other steps to deliverance. Without conversion to the Faith in Jesus Christ and participation in His family, the Church, deliverance, even if seemingly effective for a while, cannot be successful in the long run. It is the *"Truth"* that makes us free (John 8:31b), not prayers, rituals, counseling, or personal will in themselves. It is the confrontation with Truth that sends the demons running back to hell. This is why the method of Deliverance Counseling we use is called a *"Truth Encounter"*. As demons are confronted with the Truth, and as we are confronted with the Truth, of whom we are in Christ, we gain freedom. The foundation of all truth is Jesus Christ, who is Truth (John 14:6). Without our Lord Jesus Christ, we can never know truth or obtain it.

Some people believe they are unable to make a profession of faith in Jesus Christ. In such cases the person should ask God for help—ask Him for the faith that will save, deliver, and heal.

If we are willing to accept the gift of faith from God, our Lord will give it to us when we ask:

And I tell you, Ask, and it will be given you; seek, and you will find; knock, and it will be opened to you. For every one who asks receives, and he who seeks finds, and to him who knocks it will be opened. What father among you, if his son asks for a fish, will instead of a fish give him a serpent; or if he asks for an egg, will give him a scorpion? If you then, who are evil, know how to give good gifts to your children, how much more will the heavenly Father give the Holy Spirit to those who ask him! — (Luke 11:9-13)

Sincerely ask God for the faith that brings saving faith, the faith of conversion to the One, that is Jesus Christ, whom who declares:

I am the way, and the truth, and the life; no one comes to the Father, but by me (John 14:6) .... Come to me, all who labor and are heavy laden, and I will give you rest (Matthew 11:28) .... I will not reject anyone who comes to me (John 6:37) .... [rather] take my yoke upon you, and learn from me; for I am gentle and lowly in heart, and you will find rest for your souls. For my yoke is easy, and my burden is light (Matt 11:29-30)

Step 2 — Repentance

Essential to growing closer to God in faith, devotion, and love is to repent of those behaviors, desires, beliefs, and ideas that are sinful. The definition of sin is much broader than most people imagine. A definition of sin:

Sin is an offense against reason, truth, and right conscience; it is a failure in genuine love for God and neighbor caused by a perverse attachment to certain goods. Its wounds the nature of man and injures human solidarity. It has been defined as "an utterance, a deed, or a desire contrary to the eternal law."

Sin is an offense against God: *"Against you, you alone, have I sinned, and done that which is evil in your sight"* (Ps 51:4). Sin sets itself against God's love for us and turns our hearts away from it. Like the first sin (of Adam and Eve), it is disobedience, a revolt against God through the will to become "like gods" (Gen 3:5), knowing and determining good and evil. Sin is thus "love of oneself even to contempt of God." In this proud self-exaltation, sin is diametrically opposed to the obedience of Jesus, which achieves our salvation (cf. Phil 2:6-9).

We must repent of our sin, but repentance involves more than merely "turning away" from sin. Repentance must also renounce all that opposes God and all that He finds sinful. This includes renouncing Satan and his ways, renouncing personal sins, and renouncing all that leads us to sin. Some of the common sins and situations that interfere with deliverance include: involvement in non-Christian activities like the occult; persistent situational sins such as living together without marriage or remarriage without annulment of previous marriages; maintaining improper or problematic friendships; illegal activities of any sort; and sins that have become habitual such as pornography, masturbation, fornication, gossip, lying, stealing, etc.

The three greatest stumbling blocks to deliverance is Pride, Rebellion, and Unforgiveness and all the things that go along with those three sins. Repentance of Pride, Rebellion, and Unforgiveness is required to even hope for deliverance. Repentance also includes the firm amendment to avoid sin, and the near occasion of sin, in the future. Repentance requires a *complete* turnaround of our lives, a becoming a *"new man"*, so that...

...you should put away the old self of your former way of life, corrupted through deceitful desires, and be renewed in the spirit of your minds, and put on the new self, created in God's way in righteousness and holiness of truth. Therefore, putting away falsehood, speak the truth, each one to his neighbor, for we are members one of another...(thus) do not leave room for the devil (Eph 4:22-25,26b)

Step 3 — Confession

With faith and contrition of heart, repentance of mind, firm purpose to avoid sin and that which leads us to sin, we must now confess our sins before our God who is a God of forgiveness and mercy. This is a critical step that we will discuss at length.

The manner of our confession differs, but within our respective traditions, confession is required:

If we confess our sins, he is faithful and just, and will forgive our sins and cleanse us from all unrighteousness. (1 John 1:9)

... if you confess with your mouth that Jesus is Lord and believe in your heart that God raised him from the dead, you will be saved. For one believes with the heart and so is justified, and one confesses with the mouth and so is saved. (Romans 10:9-10)

"Confess your sins to each other and pray for each other so that you may be healed. The earnest prayer of a righteous person has great power and wonderful results" (James 5:16).

This confidant maybe one's pastor or another minister, or a trusted friend. We must be careful when choosing an "accountability partner." Since we will be revealing very private and sensitive information about ourselves, it is critically important to trust whoever we choose as a confidant to be discreet and to keep absolutely confidential the information we tell them.

There is wisdom in presenting oneself to an "accountability partner." Personal accountability is upheld when we confess to another person whom may hold us accountable for our actions. Confessing our sins to one another is a powerful way to break the bonds of sin in our lives. It is much harder to confess our sins to one another than to simply say, *"Lord, forgive me"*. While God is forgiving, of course, it is the demands of personal accountability before another human being that brings our confession into grounded reality that strengthens our commitment to turn away from sin in the future.

Religious ministers, psychologists, counselors, and others including the Deliverance Counselors of agency, are also bound either by law, ethical codes, or contract with the client (or bound by any combination thereof) to keep private and confidential all that is revealed to them. In addition, those in the ministerial and helping professions are usually trained in the ethics, legalities, and culture of maintaining confidentiality. They are use to keeping private the personal information of their patients and clients. Friends, on the other hand, may not have such training and may not be use to the culture of confidentiality. Thus, if one's confidant is not a pastor, or at least a minister, psychologist, or counselor bound by law and/or ethical codes, take care to ensure the chosen confidant understands thoroughly that he must keep private all that he hears and may not discuss it with anyone, not even with his spouse.

There is a great psychological comfort in hearing the words, "I forgive you" or the equivalent, "I absolve you of your sins." Our Father in heaven understands this psychological need. Thus, in His great love for us, He provided a way for us to hear those words in His name. It is God who ultimately forgives sins, but God, according to His sovereign authority chose to delegate this authority to His validly ordained priests. This power was given to the Apostles in John 20:22-23 and was passed on from them to those whom they appointed.

Our Father in heaven also knows and understands our need to be a family and for the family to come to our aid when we are hurting, to offer forgiveness when we fall, and to provide healing and strength to help us grow in faith. God forgives you when you appeal to Him with your heart-felt and sincere repentance and confession. Follow the tradition of your denomination and always offer a prayer for forgiveness as soon as possible after sinning. Then, in obedience to the Bible, seek accountability by confession to a confidant to complete your healing.

Step 4 — Removing the Greatest Stumbling blocks: Pride, Rebellion, and Forgiveness

We have already mentioned that the three biggest stumbling blocks to deliverance is usually Pride, Rebellion, and Unforgiveness. These three sins distance us from God. To draw closer to God we need to give up our pride, obey our Lord's teachings, and forgive those who hurt us.

In Deliverance Counseling we help our clients through exercises to locate pockets of pride and rebellion and to rid themselves of these sins with the help of God through prayer. Forgiveness, however, tends to be the most difficult, partly because of pride or even rebellion perhaps, but mostly because of deeply emotional issues surrounding the circumstances of the hurts someone has given us. Whatever the causes of our unforgiveness, deliverance is not possible until we can come to forgive, thus we shall discuss this topic at some length too.

The following guide is rather long, but this step is one of the most important. One simple MUST deals with Pride, Rebellion, and Unforgiveness if deliverance and healing is to be permanently possible.

Pride: Pride is the essential sin that leads to most other sins. It is the sin of Lucifer that led him to rebel against God resulting in his expulsion from heaven and becoming Satan.

Pride is a killer. Pride says, "I can do it! I can get myself out of this mess without God and without anyone else's helped." No, we can't! We absolutely need God, and we desperately need each other.

Pride also says "I know the best and most efficient way and how dare others get in the way of that" or "How dare things not go my way" or "How dare some person or something get in the way of what I want to do." Impatience is a factor of pride. Other ways impatience reveals our pride is getting impatient when we cannot find our car keys, or when we are late to a meeting, or if someone is driving too slowly for us on the hi-way, or when the computer acts up and interrupts our train of thought.

Impatience is the sister to Pride because it is caused essentially by our desire to have things our own way, in our own time, and according to our own preferences.

Pride is also the engine behind egotism (thinking more of oneself than one ought) and behind false humility (putting oneself down to be less than what one actually is). Pride is the force behind resistance to lawful and appropriate authority — whether that authority is a parent, teacher, police officer, government, employer, or the Church.

Pride is the basis of thinking of oneself as better than others, being pompous, and having contempt toward one's neighbors, employers, other family members, or the Church and her ministers.

Pride can also rear its ugly head in more subtle ways such as reluctance to apologize when we need to apologize, demanding our rights merely because it is our right, being inappropriately unkind or rude, jealousy, being quick-tempered, moodiness, brooding over wrongs done by others to oneself, depression and despair, or demanding that we are right about something, when indeed we are right about the issue, even though the issue is unimportant or can be handled differently (this is a major phenomenon in marriages, families, and friendships — the phrase "We need to choose our battles" is an important remedy for this).

Other ways that Pride expresses itself include: by taking personal credit for gifts or possessions and thus refusing to acknowledge that we have what we have by God's Providence; glorying in our achievements as if they were not primary a result of God's grace and divine goodness; by minimizing one's defeats; by claiming qualities that are not actually possessed; magnifying the faults and defects of others or dwelling upon the defects and faults of others.

James 4:6-10 and 1 Peter 5:1-10 reveals that spiritual conflict follows pride.

Examine yourself for these and any other attributes of pride and then pray:

Dear Heavenly Father. You have said that pride goes before destruction and an arrogant spirit before stumbling (Prov. 16:18). I confess that I have not denied myself, picked up my cross daily, and followed You (Matt. 16:24). In so doing I have given ground to the enemy in my life. I have believed that I could be successful and live victoriously by my own strength and resources. I now confess that I have sinned against You by placing my will before You and by centering my life around self instead of You.

I now renounce the self-life and by so doing cancel all the ground that has been gained in my life by the enemies of the Lord Jesus Christ. I pray that You will guide me so that I will do nothing from selfishness or empty conceit, but with humility of mind that I will regard others as more important than myself (Phil. 2:3). Enable me through love to serve others and in honor prefer others (Rom. 12:10). Amen.

Rebellion: We often place our confidence in the flesh not only with the "I can do it myself" attitude but each time we assert our own opinions above the teachings of Christ. It is a pride and a rebellion to say, "I want to do it my way" or "I want to think the way I want" without regard to the ways God teaches us to go and to believe. This is an arrogance that not only can get us into major trouble but also forms a major vulnerability for demons to come into our life.

Rebelling against God and His authority gives Satan an opportunity to attack. As our commanding general, the Lord Jesus Christ says, *"Get into ranks and follow Me. I will not lead you into temptation, but I will deliver you from evil."*

The Bible teaches us that it is the will of God for us to be obedient to parents, to civil government, to the Church, and to the pastors who are over us. We have two biblical responsibilities in regard to these authority figures: 1) Pray for them; and 2) submit to them. The only time God permits us to disobey those in authority over us is when they require of us an act or acquiescence in ways that are contrary to Church Law, Natural Law, or Divine Law.

Being under authority is an act of faith; we are trusting God to work through His established lines of authority. The authority that God has ordained does not mean, however, that we are to submit to abuse from those authorities. In those cases where someone in authority over us is abusing us in any way, then we need to act in appropriate ways according to the situation — such as appeal to the state for protection and relief for civil or criminal issues; or appeal to Church authorities on some issue involving religion or our parish; or make appropriate decisions such as terminating an abusive relationship, etc. Whoever the authority, who is abusing, we need to pray for the offender and to forgive him; but we are not required to be a doormat or target of their abuse.

Some of the lines of authority mentioned in the Bible include:

- Church leaders (Hebrews 13:17; Matthew 18:15-18)
- Parents (Ephesians 6: 1-3; Exodus 20:12)
- Husbands (1 Peter 3:1-3; Ephesians 5:23-24)
- Employers (1 Peter 2:18-21)
- Civil Government (Romans 13:1-5; 1 Timothy 2:1-3; 1 Peter 2:13-16)

Examine yourself for any areas of rebellion (deliberate driving faster than the speed limit is rebellion, too, you know!) and then pray:

Dear Heavenly Father. You have said that rebellion is as the sin of witchcraft and insubordination is as iniquity and idolatry (1 Sam. 15.23). I know that in action and attitude I have sinned against You with a rebellious heart. I ask Your forgiveness for my rebellion and pray that by the shed blood of the Lord Jesus Christ, strengthened by intercession of the that all ground gained by evil spirits because of my rebelliousness be canceled and taken back. I pray that You will shed light on all my ways that I may know the full extent of my rebelliousness, and I now choose to adopt a submissive spirit and a servant's heart. Amen.

Unforgiveness: Jesus Himself discusses the seriousness of failing to forgive. He tells us that failure to forgive those who hurt us will result in our not being forgiven ourselves by God. *"Forgive us our trespasses (sins) as we forgive those who trespass (sin) against us"*. The *Our Father*, the Lord's Prayer, which most all of us know and pray, Jesus teaches us that God will be as forgiving to us as we are to others.

Indeed, how can we expect God to forgive us when we do not forgive our brothers? Consider the follow teachings from Holy Scripture:

If you forgive those who sin against you, your heavenly Father will forgive you. But if you refuse to forgive others, your Father will not forgive your sins (Matthew 6:14,15).

But when you are praying, first forgive anyone you are holding a grudge against, so that your Father in heaven will forgive your sins, too (Mark 11:25).

If you forgive others, you will be forgiven. (Luke 6:37b)

Forgiveness is not about emotions and feelings. You can still be hurting, angry and upset and still decide to forgive. Forgiveness involves a mental decision, a decision of will, an act of your free will, even though you may not "Feel it".

The true nature of forgiveness:

1. **Forgiveness is not forgetting:** People who try to forget find that cannot. It is an unfortunate quirk of the English language with the phrase, "Forgive and forget". In actuality this phrase does not mean to "forget" in the sense of not remembering what happened; of course, we will remember. God says He will "remember our sins no more" (Heb. 10: 17), but God, being omniscient, obviously cannot literally forget. "Remember no more" means that God will never use the past against us (Ps. 103:12).

   To forget is really "to let go". We need to *"let go and let God"*. We let go of the past, but more importantly we let go of the hurt. As long as we do not forgive, as long as we do not let go, we allow the offender of our wounds continue to hurt us.

2. **Forgiveness is a choice not a feeling:** Since God requires us to forgive, <u>it is something we can do</u>. God will NEVER ask us to do something that is impossible for us to do; that would be cruel and God is a loving God.

   Forgiveness, however, is difficult for us because it pulls against our feelings and emotional hurts. Forgiveness is not about forgetting our feelings or our emotional hurts. We often will not "feel" like forgiving, but we must forgive anyway. As the Lord Prayer teaches us, God forgives us "as we forgive others". But how can God require this of us when we have been hurt so badly?

God does not expect your feelings and emotional hurts to be healed overnight. He knows and understands our feelings and our hurts. He is a compassionate God and will help us to heal over time, as we are able. What God expects of us is not an immediate emotional healing, but a decision of will to forgive, a decision of will to trust Him to take care of the offender and to heal us, a decision of will to ask God for, and to commit to, being healed of our wounds.

3. **Forgiveness is not letting the person off the hook:** Forgiving is about you letting go, but it is not letting the offender off the hook. He will still pay for what he did, either before the Law or before God or both.

Forgiving is surely difficult for us because it pulls against our concept of justice. We want revenge for offenses suffered. But we are told never to take our own revenge (Rom. 12:9). Revenge does more damage to us than it punishes the offender. God's justice will prevail, no one can escape it. Never fear, those who hurt us will be held accountable, but we must let God deal with it. In order for God to deal with it, we need to let Him deal with it by letting go.

"Why should I let them off the hook?" But doing that is precisely the problem — we are still hooked to them, still bound by our past when we do not forgive.

To forgive does not mean letting the person off the hook; it means letting yourself off the hook.

4. **But you don't understand how much this person hurt me:** The problem is that when we do not forgive we, in essence, allow the person to still hurt us! The question is, "How do we stop the pain?" The answer is **to forgive!**

It is important to understand that we do not forgive someone for their sake; we do it for our sake so we can be free. Our need to forgive is not an issue between the offender and us; it is between us and God.

5. **Forgiveness is agreeing to live with the consequences of another's sin:** Forgiveness is costly. We pay the price of the evil we forgive. We are going to live with those consequences whether we want to or not; our only choice is whether or not we will do so in the slavery of bitterness and unforgiveness or with the freedom of forgiveness.

Jesus took the consequences of our sin upon Himself. All true forgiveness is substitution because no one really forgives without bearing the consequences of the other person's sin. God the Father *"made Him who knew no sin to be sin on our behalf, that we might become the righteousness of God in Him"* (2 Cor. 5:2 1).

Where is the justice? We might ask. It is the Cross that makes forgiveness legally and morally right: *"For the death that He died, He died to sin, once for all"* (Rom. 6: 10). This doesn't mean that we tolerate sin. We must always stand against sin, but we must give the offender to God and get on with our life.

6. **How do we forgive from our heart?** First, we acknowledge the hurt and the hate. If our forgiveness does not visit the emotional core of our life, it will be incomplete. Many feel the pain of interpersonal offenses, but they will not acknowledge it. Let God bring the pain to the surface so He can deal with it. This is where the healing takes place.

   Do not wait to forgive until we feel like forgiving; we will never get there. Feelings take time to heal mostly <u>after</u> the choice to forgive is made and Satan has lost his place (Eph. 4:26, 27). Freedom is what will be gained, not a feeling.

7. **Summary of Points on Forgiveness:**
   - Forgiveness is necessary to have fellowship with God.
   - It is not forgetting.
   - It is a choice.
   - Letting the offender off <u>our</u> hook is what frees us.
   - The offender is not off God's hook.
   - God says, "Revenge is mine."
   - You must acknowledge the hurt and the hate.
   - Forgiveness means we are agreeing to live with the consequences of another's sin — which we have to do anyway.
   - The justice is in the cross.
   - Choice is between the slavery of bitterness or the freedom of forgiveness.
   - Forgiveness means not using the past against the offender.
   - Forgiveness <u>does not</u> mean tolerating the sin or abuse.
   - Why forgive? To stop the pain! As we live in unforgiveness the offender still hurts us!
   - The issue of forgiveness is between you and God only.
   - The act of forgiveness is for your sake, and for your freedom.

Think about the people in your life for whom you need to forgive, people to whom you hold bitterness, people who have hurt you or disappointed you in anyway, or for whom you hold any kind of grudge. Be sure to ALWAYS include your parents, siblings, spouse, and YOURSELF. There is always something to forgive in our families and in ourselves.

Record all the names you can think of on a sheet of paper and a brief note as to why you need to forgive them. If you do not remember names, list them by what you do remember, such as "the guy in sixth grade with the red hat". If you cannot remember why you need to forgive someone on your list that is okay; forgive them for whatever it was — God knows.

After preparing this list ask God to bring to your mind anyone you have forgotten. It is not unusual to forget, or to push aside from our conscious mind, incidents and even the names of people whom have hurt us. These hidden hurts and wounds need to be healed as well. Thus, ask God to bring to your mind any person you have forgotten for whom you need to forgive, for whom you hold a grudge against, for which you are bitter, for those who have hurt you, with the following prayer:

Father in heaven, please bring to my mind the names of any people for whom I have held bitterness towards, grudges against, or have not forgiven for the hurts they have caused me. Help me to remember all these hurts so that they may be offered to You, O Lord, and healed from my soul so that I may live the truly victorious Christ-life. Amen.

Add to your list the names of anyone God may bring to your mind.

Now it is time to pray...

The following prayer needs to be said for each person on the list for which you need to forgive. Do not go to the next person on the list until you are sure you have dealt with all the remembered pain.

As you pray, God may bring to your mind various offending people and experiences that has been totally forgotten. Allow God to do this even if it is painful. Remember this process of forgiveness is for your sake because God wants you to be free.

Remember also that by forgiving the offender we are not rationalizing or trying to explain the offender's behavior. Forgiveness deals with the victim's pain, your pain, not another's excuses. Positive feelings will follow in time; freeing you from the past is the critical issue now.

If you are willing to forgive for your sake, so that you can walk away from this webpage free in Christ, free from the past and from person who hurt you, pray the introductory prayer below and then pray the "Prayer to Forgive" for each person on your list:

Heavenly Father, I now ask for your help in forgiving all those people on my list. Although I am still hurt and angry with them, I know that they are your children and that you love them more than I can possibly know. For this reason, my God, I ask you to help me forgive them. I lay down all bitterness, resentment and hatred for this person and I freely choose to forgive them. Teach me to be more merciful, my God, and help me be always willing, just as you are always willing, to forgive those who sin against me. Amen."

Prayer to Forgive

Lord, I forgive _________________________________ for (specifically identify all offenses and painful memories).

May God heal you and bless you!

Step 5 — Know Who You Are in Christ!

In order to gain freedom, it is important to know who you are in Christ. Thus, you need to evaluate the concept you have of yourself, to acknowledge the truth about God and about yourself; about your relationship and ideas about God and about the manner of our lives.

We often deceive ourselves about our position in Christ and our relationship with Him. For example, we may say to ourselves: "This isn't going to work" or "I wish I could believe this but I can't" or perhaps even more direct deceptions or denials concerning the promises of God for His children. Areas of deception that we may have include:

1. **Self-Deception** (telling ourselves things that are not true)
   - Listening to God's words but thinking we do not have to do it (Ja 1:22; 4:17)
   - Thinking we have no sin or do not sin (1 Jn 1:8)
   - Thinking that we are something when we are not (Gal 6:3)
   - Believing that we will not reap what we sow (Gal 6:7)
   - Thinking we are wise and sophisticated in the 21st century (1 Cor 3:18, 19)
   - Believing that the unrighteous will reach heaven (1 Cor 6:9)
   - Thinking we can associate with bad company and not be corrupted (1 Cor 15:33)
2. **Self-Defense** (defending ourselves instead of trusting Christ)
   - Denial (conscious or subconscious)
   - Fantasy (escape from the real world)
   - Emotional insulation (withdraw to avoid rejection)
   - Regression (reverting back to a less threatening time in the past)
   - Displacement (taking out frustrations on others)
   - Projection (blaming others or accusing others of things we ourselves have done)
   - Rationalization (defending self though verbal excursion)

To counter these and other deceptions we tell ourselves we need to exercise faith. Faith is the response to Truth and believing the truth is a CHOICE (not a feeling). If we say, "I want to believe God, but I just can't," then we are deceiving ourselves. Of course, we can believe God. We know that God does not lie. Faith is something we DECIDE to do; it is not something we FEEL like doing. Believing the truth does not make it true; rather it is TRUE, therefore we believe it.

Examine yourself and how you may deceive yourself with "self-deceptions" and "Self-Defense" mechanisms. The pray the following prayer: ...

Prayer to Know the Truth:

Dear Heavenly Father. I know that You desire truth in the inner self and that facing this truth is the way of liberation (John 8:32). I acknowledge that I have been deceived by the father of lies (John 8:44) and that I have deceived myself (1 John 1:8). I pray in the name of the Lord Jesus Christ, and since by faith I have received You into my life and am now seated with Christ in the heavenliest (Eph 2:6), I ask you Father to command all deceiving spirits to depart from me. I now ask You to *"search me, O God, and know my heart: try me and know my anxious thoughts;*

and see if there be any hurtful way in me, and lead me in the everlasting way" (Ps. 139:23, 24)
In the name of Christ Jesus I pray. Amen.

Knowing the truth about oneself, overcoming self-deceptions and the mechanism of self-defense that hide who we really are, includes understanding our faith in Christ. It is by Christ that our lives have meaning and substance.

The following prayer is the substance of that faith:

Affirmations

I believe that I am a child of God (1 Jn. 3:1-3) and that I am seated with Christ in the heavenlies (Eph. 2:6). I believe that I was saved by the grace of God through faith that is a gift and not the result of my own efforts or merits (Eph 2:8).

I choose to be strong in the Lord and in the strength of His might (Eph 6:10). I put no confidence in the flesh (Phil 3:3) for the weapons of warfare are not of the flesh (2 Cor. 10:4). I put on the whole armor of God (Eph. 6:10-20), and I resolve to stand firm in my faith and to resist the evil one.

I believe that Jesus Christ has all authority in heaven and on earth (Matt 28:18) and that He is the head over all rule and authority (Col 2:10). I believe that Satan and his demons and wicked spirits are subject to the Lord Jesus Christ and therefore to me in Christ since I am a member of Christ's body (Eph 1:19-23).

I believe that apart from Christ I can do nothing (John 15:5) so I declare my dependence upon Him.

I choose to abide in Christ in order to bear much fruit and to glorify the Lord (Jn 15:8) and to accomplish the work of sanctification that Christ began in me through the Cross (James 2).

I believe that since I am a member go God's royal family I have the authority, in the name of Christ Jesus, to ask the Father to command the devil to leave my presence, as I obey the command to resist the devil (James 4:7).

I reject any counterfeit gifts or works of Satan and his minions in my life.

I believe that the truth will set me free (John 8:32) and that walking in the light is the only path of fellowship and freedom (1 John 1:7). Therefore, as a royal member of God's household, I stand against Satan's deceptions by affirming all the doctrines of the Faith and by taking every thought captive in obedience to Christ (2 Cor 10:5).

I declare that the Bible and the Church are the only authoritative standards for me (2 Tim 3:15, 16).

I choose to speak the truth in love (Eph 4:15).

I choose to present my body as an instrument of righteousness, a living and holy sacrifice, and thus I renew my mind daily by the living Word of God in order that I may prove that the will of God is good, acceptable, and perfect (Rom 6:13; 12:1, 2).

I ask my heavenly Father to fill me with His Holy Spirit (Eph 5:18), to lead me into all truth (John 16:13), and to empower my life that I may live above sin and not carry out the desires of the flesh (Gal 5:16). I crucify the flesh (Gal 5:24) and choose to walk by the Spirit.

In making all these affirmations, I renounce all selfish goals and choose the ultimate goal of love (1 Tim 1:5). I choose to obey the greatest commandment to love the Lord my God will all my heart, soul, and mind, and to love my neighbor as myself (Matt 22:37-39). Amen.

Step 6 — Worship, Pray, and Fast

Worship as a Church Family: One of Satan's favorite lies, apart from having us believe that he does not exist, or that he does exist and is more powerful than he truly is, is that since God is everywhere and we can worship Him anywhere and do not need the "community of believers ", the Church family.

Although it is true that God is everywhere and worshiping Him anywhere is wholesome and good, it is false to believe that the Church is unnecessary. Since the earliest days of Christianity, communities of believers gathered together on the *Lord's Day* (Sunday).

Scripture is very clear on the subject of Church attendance and on how our submission to its authority is not only good but required. The Church, its leaders and members, are the Mystical Body of Christ here on Earth. To disobey the teachings of the Church as it relates to faith and morals is to disobey the teachings of Christ. To not attend church is also disobedience to Christ.

Paul admonishes those who do not come to Church in Hebrews 10:19-25:

Therefore, brothers, since through the blood of Jesus we have confidence of entrance into the sanctuary by the new and living way he opened for us through the veil, that is, his flesh, and since we have "a great priest over the house of God," let us approach with a sincere heart and in absolute trust, with our hearts sprinkled clean from an evil conscience and our bodies washed in pure water. Let us hold unwaveringly to our confession that gives us hope, for he who made the promise is trustworthy. We must consider how to rouse one another to love and good works. We should not stay away from our assembly, as is the custom of some, but encourage one another, and this all the more as you see the day drawing near.

Hebrews 13:17

Obey your leaders and submit to them; for they are keeping watch over your souls, as men who will have to give account. Let them do this joyfully, and not sadly, for that would be of no advantage to you.

Worship and prayer together as a family, prayer meetings, adoration, and other corporate settings, and in the privacy of the family at home is critical in developing spiritual health for the family and each family member. Such family devotion forms the foundation for all that each family does away from home in the world of school, work, and society.

Prayer is so important both in the family context and individually. It is important not just because prayer is something a Christian ought to do, but because prayer is communication.

The more we depend on God, the closer He is to us and we are to Him. Aligning ourselves with God, communicating with Him at all times and in all situations and personal decisions will unite our hearts to His. A heart united to the Creator will overflow with graces and blessings.

Prayer and Spiritual Warfare: In addition, a healthy prayer life destroys strongholds that demons may have in our lives and in our hearts. Without prayer we cannot hope to be delivered from spiritual afflictions. It is no secret —prayer, worship, devotion, and living the Christ-Life in all that it entails is the formula not only for deliverance from spiritual afflictions, but for living the victorious life in Christ.

When dealing with spiritual afflictions, however, some special prayer considerations may be needed. Scripture states that there are certain demons that will only respond to prayer as well as fasting: *"But this kind does not go out except by prayer and fasting."* (Matthew 17:21). If fasting can defeat even the strongest of fallen angels, just how powerful is this sacrifice that we can make?

Spiritual warfare prayers are very effective in defeating the enemy and drawing our hearts closer to God.

Step 7 — Live the Faith and Remain Faithful

Along with all the advice and recommendations of the first six steps, our healing and deliverance cannot be complete unless we act upon our faith. Doing good works and charitable acts of love are a natural outflow of our faith and necessary to lead a good Christian life. It is not enough to believe. James asks and admonishes in James 2:19,20, 26:

Do you still think it's enough just to believe that there is one God? Well, even the demons believe this, and they tremble in terror! Fool! When will you ever learn that faith that does not result in good deeds is useless?

Just as the body is dead without a spirit, so also faith is dead without good deeds.

James calls a man a fool who does not act upon his faith in James 1:22-25:

Be doers of the word and not hearers only, deluding yourselves. For if anyone is a hearer of the Word and not a doer, he is like a man who looks at his own face in a mirror. He sees himself, then goes off and promptly forgets what he looks like. But the one who peers into the prefect law of freedom and perseveres, and is not a hearer who forgets but a doer who acts, such a one shall be blessed in what he does.

It is hard to live the Christ-Life, but we must try. We must not have a faith that is dead and useless. We must not be a fool and not practice our faith. We must, rather, live out our faith and persevere in the faith:

1 Corinthians 9:23-27

All this I do for the sake of the gospel, so that I too may have a share in it. Do you not know that the runners in the stadium all run in the race, but only one wins the prize? Run so as to win. Every athlete exercises discipline in every way. They do it to win a perishable crown, but we an imperishable one. Thus, I do not run aimlessly; I do not fight as if I were shadowboxing. No, I drive my body and train it, for fear that, after having preached to others, I myself should be disqualified.

Colossians 1:17-23

He is before all things, and in him all things hold together. He is the head of the body, the church. He is the beginning, the firstborn from the dead, that in all things he himself might be preeminent. For in him all the fullness was pleased to dwell, and through him to reconcile all things for him, making peace by the blood of his cross (through him), whether those on earth or those in heaven.

And you who once were alienated and hostile in mind because of evil deeds he has now reconciled in his fleshly body through his death, to present you holy, without blemish, and irreproachable before him, provided that you persevere in the faith, firmly grounded, stable, and not shifting from the hope of the gospel that you heard, which has been preached to every creature under heaven, of which I, Paul, am a minister.

And thus, let us be able to say, with St. Paul, in 2 Timothy 4:6-8

For I am already on the point of being sacrificed; the time of my departure has come. I have fought the good fight, I have finished the race, I have kept the faith. Henceforth there is laid up for me the crown of righteousness, which the Lord, the righteous judge, will award to me on that Day, and not only to me but also to all who have loved His appearing.

Persevere in the faith and let your life be a living Gospel for you shall thereby *know the truth and the truth shall set you free*

I have outlined steps detailing certain issues that we have found important in gaining freedom for a person in spiritual affliction.

1. purify one's conscience by a good confession;
2. Receive Holy Communion as often as possible;
3. Implore the mercy of God by prayer and fasting.
4. Recourse to specific spiritual warfare prayers applicable to the situation.

Final Thoughts

Repentance, forgiveness, acting on our faith, praying, fasting, receiving the Sacrament frequently, and all the rest we ought to do as good Christians are very good things and very necessary for this life, but more importantly for the life to come.

The advice contained in these Steps to Self-Deliverance, however, are not "quick fixes". This advice involves a lifelong commitment for anyone with spiritual afflictions. Freeing yourself from the bondages of the enemy and keeping them from returning requires this commitment to persevere in Christ and in the Christ-life.

There will be dry times. Your faith will be tested. Indeed, the demons may (and more than likely will) try to return. Scripture speaks of what demons do once they are cast out:

Now when the unclean spirit goes out of a man, it passes through waterless places seeking rest, and does not find it. Then it says, 'I will return to my house from which I came'; and when it comes, it finds it unoccupied, swept, and put in order. Then it goes and takes along with it seven other spirits more wicked than itself, and they go in and live there; and the last state of that man becomes worse than the first. (Matthew 12, 43-45).

Do not leave your house (heart) *"unoccupied, swept and put in order"*; rather be filled with the Holy Spirit.

We can never let down our guard. As a final instruction, remember the teaching of St. Paul in Ephesians 6:10-18. We do not go about our day without putting on our clothes. Do not go into the world with God's armor:

Finally, draw your strength from the Lord and from his mighty power. Put on the armor of God so that you may be able to stand firm against the tactics of the devil. For our struggle is not with flesh and blood but with the principalities, with the powers, with the world rulers of this present darkness, with the evil spirits in the heavens. Therefore, put on the armor of God that you may be able to resist on the evil day and, having done everything, to hold your ground. So, stand fast with your loins girded in truth, clothed with righteousness as a breastplate, and your feet shod in readiness for the gospel of peace. In all circumstances, hold faith as a shield, to quench all (the) flaming arrows of the evil one. And take the helmet of salvation and the sword of the Spirit, which is the word of God. With all prayer and supplication, pray at every opportunity in the Spirit. To that end, be watchful with all perseverance and supplication.

APENDEX 1
Steps for Self-Deliverance

The purpose of all this information is to enable you to do a self-deliverance at home for yourself. The process of self-deliverance is carried out in stages. Let's go through them one by one.

STEP ONE: Start with praise and worship. You can sing songs to praise God and to worship Him.

STEP TWO: Confess out loud Scriptures promising deliverance. Luke 10:19, Ephesians 1:7, Romans 16:20, Revelation 12:11, Colossians 2:14-15, Galatians 3:13-14, Psalms 91:3…*2 Timothy 4:18* says And the Lord shall deliver me from every evil work, and will preserve me unto His heavenly kingdom: to whom be glory forever and ever. Amen. You should memorize *2 Tim 4:18*.

STEP THREE: Break covenants and curses to destroy their legal hold. You pray a simple prayer like this: I break any curse or covenant working against me, in the name of Jesus. (Simple prayers)

STEP FOUR: Bind all the spirits associated with those covenants and curses like this: I bind all the spirits attached or connected to the curses and covenants I have just broken, in the name of Jesus.

STEP FIVE: Lay one hand on your head and pray, Holy Ghost, cover me from the top of my head to the sole of my feet, in the name of Jesus. Begin to mention every organ of your body; kidney, liver, intestine, blood, etc. You must not rush at this level. Lay your hands-on areas that the Spirit of God leads you to.

STEP SIX: Then begin to saturate yourself with the Blood of Jesus. You do this by saying: I plead the Blood of Jesus over me. This must continue until you have a release in your spirit to stop.

STEP SEVEN: It is now, that you can demand firmly, in the name of the Lord Jesus Christ, that any spirit that is not of God should leave you. You demand it forcefully like this: In the name of the Lord Jesus Christ, I come against all you hidden spirits and I bind your activities in my life. You can no longer hide below the surface because I now recognize what you have been doing; release me, in the name of Jesus.

(If sickness is the problem, address it and say) You spirit of infirmity, I speak to you directly, get out of my life now. I am redeemed by the Blood of Jesus Christ, come out and go now. Go out with every breath by the power of the Holy Spirit. I prevail over you, in the name of Jesus.

STEP EIGHT: Ask for a fresh in-filling of the Holy Spirit and close the session with praises. Self-deliverance keeps you from getting sick; it removes every evil seed of the enemy; it charges your body with fire. It uproots evil plantations and builds up your confidence. Every night before you go to bed, you must remember these two important prayer points.

1. Pray for cover with the Blood of Jesus. ***Revelation 12:11*** = And they overcame him by the Blood of the Lamb, and by the word of their testimony; and they loved not their lives unto the death.
2. Pray that the Angels of God should surround you. ***Psalms 34:7*** = The Angel of the Lord encampeth round about them that fear him, and delivereth them.

No matter how sleepy you are, make sure pray these two prayer points every night. There is no reason why self-deliverance should not be effective. However, if the person seeking deliverance is under stubborn demonic control or hereditary strongman and lacks sufficient faith or authority to defeat the oppressors or living in any known sin, the evil spirits will be hard to get rid of. right.

One final word of caution. For a person to be delivered, he/she must want deliverance. Self-deliverance must not be done because of pride, shyness, the fear of possible public embarrassment, etc. Your motive for engaging in self-deliverance has to be pure.

REMEMBER: ***DELIVERANCE IS A PROCESS (((NOT A ONE-TIME EVENT)))*** AND THE LENGTH OF TIME IT TAKES DEPENDS ON SEVERAL THINGS;

1. The length of time the spirit has stayed inside a person
2. The strength and reinforcement of the spirit
3. The experience and degree of anointing upon those who are ministering the deliverance
4. The willingness of the person being delivered to be free
5. The knowledge of the Word of God and your level of hatred for sin
6. SELF-DISCIPLINE IS NECESSARY

Also, remember that bondage can be weak or strong. A weak hold can be broken quickly, whereas a stronghold may take a more time. You will not realize the strength of bondage until you faithfully and persistently work on it. You must remember that a foothold can graduate to a stronghold if left unaddressed. After this exercise, set aside some days (with fasting). DO NOT CONTINUE TO DO THE THINGS THAT CAUSED THE "it"! CHANGE YOUR HABITS TO AGREE WITH YOUR PRAYERS. AMEN.

Appendix 2

Exposing the Doors to Bondage

Part I: The bondage

1. When did this bondage start?

2. Was there any unusual things that took place (or you did) when this bondage started?

3. If this bondage started when you were a child: Do you have ancestors who have suffered from a similar kind of bondage?

4. What kind of bondage are you facing? (Fears, depression, voices in your mind, mental illness, physical illness, mental torment, spiritual torment, etc... Please be as detailed as possible.)

5. What are all the things that have impacted your life? (Parent's death, trauma, a certain situation that changed your life, anything that 'changed' you.)

Part II: Your ancestor's background

1. Do you have ancestors who have struggled with similar problems or bondages?

2. Did your bondage start as a child and appear to have no reason to be there?

3. Do you have siblings who suffer from similar bondages or oppression?

Part III: Soul ties

1. Have you been involved with extramarital sex? Are you attracted to an ex-lover? Is he or she a good/godly influence for you?

2. Have you been divorced?

3. Do you feel an unusual attraction to a past boyfriend, girlfriend or lover (who is obviously not right for you)?

4. Do you let anybody dominate, control, or make your choices you?

5. Have you ever formed a blood covenant with another person? (Blood brothers, etc.)

6. Have you ever made vows or agreements with somebody in effort to strengthen the relationship or commit yourself to each other?

7. Do you see any ungodly relationships in your past where gifts were exchanged? (Are you holding onto something that was given to you from somebody you had adultery with, etc.)

8. Have you ever had ungodly relations with any one?

9. Do you have any pictures in your possession of somebody whom you may have an ungodly soul tie with? (A picture of you with somebody you had an adultery with, etc.)

Part IV: Relationship with parents

1. What do you think of your parents?

2. How would you explain your childhood?

3. Where you close to your parents while growing up? If not, why?

4. How would you explain your relationship with your parents? Was it good, bad or very cold?

5. Did you feel rejection from your parents?

6. Was either of your parents overly passive or controlling?

7. Has either of your parents been divorced? Remarried? Are your parents divorced?

8. How would you describe your relationship with your siblings growing up?

Part V: Rejection and abuse

1. Were your parents married when you were conceived? Were you the right sex? Did your parents not want you, or want you to be different (gender, etc.) in any way? If so, explain.

2. Did you feel rejected as a child? As an adult? If so, by whom? Explain.

3. Did you face abuse? What kind (emotional, physical, sexual, etc.) and by whom?

4. Have you faced rejection from your peers, classmates, friends or those around you?

5. Have you ever been put down, belittled, or made fun of? If so, by whom? Explain.

6. If you have faced rejection or abuse, how did you respond? Do you feel you are still paying a price for it? If so, how?

7. How do you respond to rejection right now?

8. Do you reject yourself (self-rejection)? If so, why and in what ways?

Part VI: Unforgiveness or bitterness

1. Is there anybody you feel edgy around? (Don't like them, feel anything in your heart against them, etc.)

2. Do you have anything against anybody? In other words, is there anybody that you have a hard time demonstrating the love of Christ to?

3. Has anybody wronged you that you haven't forgiven from your heart (thoughts, feelings, emotions, etc.)?

4. How do your view your siblings, parents, coworkers, etc.? Do you have any hard feelings against them?

5. Do you make a habit of blaming yourself for everything? Do you obsess over your mistakes and feel unusually guilty for them?

6. Do you deeply regret things that you've done in your past? Could you kick yourself over something you've done in your past? If so, explain.

Part VII: Personality

1. Are you a very positive or negative person?

2. Do you feel confident in yourself? If so, why?

3. Do you have a low self-esteem? If so, why?

4. Are you domineering or controlling? If so, to whom, and in what ways? Why?

5. Are you an achiever? (A go-getter) If so, in what ways?

6. Do you feel that you are always right and that if everybody did everything your way, this world would be a better place to live?

7. How do you treat your children? Husband? Are you controlling, passive, etc.?

8. Do you like people to 'look at you' (as in receive attention)?

Part VIII: Emotional health

1. Do you strive to feel accepted? If so, how does this affect your lifestyle? By whom do you want to feel accepted?

2. Are you always stressed out? If so, why?

3. Do you feel hurt? If so, by whom/what and why?

4. Do you feel good about yourself? If not, why?

5. Do you feel depressed? If so, why? When did it start? Did your parents or grandparents struggle with depression? If so, then do you know when it started and why? Do you have siblings who are also struggling? Do you feel your depression is rational or irrational?

6. Do you struggle with fears? If so, what is it that you fear? (Fear of heights, dying, being hopeless, failure, never marrying, etc.)

7. Do you worry about things? What things do you worry about? Why?

8. Do you struggle with anger? Do you have a short temper?

9. Do you have any insecurity? If so, explain.

10. Do you feel any self-pity or feel sorry for yourself? Have you ever felt this? If so, why?

11. Do you find it easy to hate people? If so, over what kinds of things would a person have to do to make you hate them?

12. Do you have any irrational feelings? If so, what are they?

13. Do you feel like something is wrong with you?

14. Do you feel excessively guilty over anything? Is this a continual problem?

15. Are you very confused and forgetful? (Beyond the normal)

16. Are you aware of any emotional wounds that have affected you?

17. Have you ever been deeply embarrassed over something? What was it?

18. Have you been in or are currently experiencing very difficult (depressing) circumstances which may cause you to feel hopeless or depressed?

Part IX: Who are you in Christ? And how do you see God?

1. How do you explain your relationship with God?

2. Do you feel you aren't good enough to meet His standards?

3. Do you see Him as a loving father, or a dictator?

4. Do you believe that it's only by the Blood of Jesus that your sins are forgiven? Or do you feel you need to earn your forgiveness in any way?

5. Do you feel God's love in your life?

6. Do you feel like your sins are forgiven? Or do you feel guilty?

7. Do you feel excessively guilty in everyday life?

8. Do you feel that doing good things, you earn God's love and acceptance?

9. Do you feel that God is angry or upset with you?

Part X: Spoken curses, vows & oaths

1. Have you ever spoken something negative about yourself that has come to past? For example: "I'm sick and tired..." or "If I don't quit typing, I'm going to get arthritis!"

2. Has your parents, or those in authority over you spoken out a curse over you? For example: "You'll never amount to anything!" or "You'll never get out of debt" or "You're so dumb"

3. Have you ever made a vow out of anger? If so, what? For example: "I'll never let anybody push me around again!" or "I'm never going to be hurt again!"

4. Have you ever wished to die? Have you ever said it?

5. If you have made any vows or oaths, what are they?

Part XI: Relationships

1. Do you have many friends? What kind of people are they?

2. Do you have a hard time trying to meet new people or make friends?

3. Are you socially outgoing or shy? If so, why?

4. How would you define your relationship with your spouse?

Part XII: Sexuality

1. Have you ever had unholy sex? What kind? (Fornication, adultery, sodomy, with a child, etc.)

2. Have you struggled with lust, fantasy or unholy sexual thoughts? If so, what kind?

3. Have you been attracted to pornography?

4. Do you have homosexual thoughts and desires? If so, have you acted upon those feelings?

5. How do you feel about your sexuality? (Do you feel dirty about it, or do you feel it's a wonderful blessing that God's given you?)

6. Do you withhold sex from your spouse or are you fidgety? Do you enjoy a healthy relationship with your spouse sexually? How does he or she react?

7. Have you ever been raped or sexually abused?

8. Have you ever woke up and felt a sexual presence with you? There are demons that imitate male and female functions, and stimulate their host (a person) sexually (beyond the normal 'wet dream').

9. Do you struggle or have you struggled with masturbation?

10. Do you struggle or have you struggled with any other sexual related thoughts, desires, or bondages?

11. Is there anything sexually that you are ashamed of?

Part XIII: Addictions

1. Do you have any addictions? If so, what kind? (Drugs, alcohol, smoking, eating, sex, TV, etc.) When did they start?

2. Did anybody else in your family (siblings, ancestors, etc.) have a struggle with any addictions? If so, what? Who?

3. Have you ever had, or currently have any sort of obsession over anything? If so, what?

Part XIV: False religions

Examples of false religions: Buddhism, Hindu, Jehovah Witness, Mormonism, Christian Scientists, eastern religions, etc.

1. Have you ever been involved with any false religions? If so, why, when and how long? How do you feel about those beliefs now?

2. Have you ever been involved in any secret societies such as Freemasonry? If so, how deep were you involved?

Part XV: The occult

1. Have you ever shown interest in the occult? If so, in what ways? (Read up on it, dabbled in it, etc.)

2. Do you still feel drawn or attracted to the occult?

3. Have you had any interest in horror or thriller style movies or novels? Are you still attracted to these things?

4. Have you ever made a vow with the devil? If so, what?

5. Married Satan?

6. Worshipped a demon or Satan?

7. Have you ever put a curse or spell on somebody?

8. Are you aware of any curses or spells placed on you? If so, what? Who did it?

9. Dabbled with an Ouija board? If so, why?

10. Ever been a member of a coven (group of 13 witches)? Explain.

11. Communicated with the dead? Explain.

12. Told somebody's fortune or went to see a fortune teller? Explain.

13. Ever read your horoscope?

14. Watched or been involved in a séance? Explain.

15. Have you been involved or a victim of Satanic Ritual Abuse (SRA)? Explain.

16. Been baptized into a false religion or any other evil baptism? If so, what were you baptized into? When?

17. Have you ever had a spirit guide?

18. Have you ever been involved with meditation, yoga, karate, or related activities?

19. Were you or anybody in your family superstitious? If so, who?

20. Ever been involved in astral travel? (Out of body)

21. If you have made any vows or oaths, what are they? Were there any sacrifices or rituals that were accompanied with them?

22. Have you ever made a blood pact before? If so, with whom (including persons, demons and Satan) and for what purpose?

23. Have you ever partaken in automatic writing, automatic drawing or automatic painting?

24. Have you ever been involved in Yoga, transcendental meditation, or similar activities?

25. Have you ever sought healing from a spiritual source other than Jesus Christ? (New age healing, energy healing, etc.)

26. Any other involvement in the occult? Explain.

Part XVI: Un-confessed sins

1. Are there any un-confessed sins that you have not repented of? (Usually something you've done, that you know is wrong, but won't admit to it. An abortion, stealing, etc. are some examples.)

2. Is there anything you've been hiding inside that you haven't confessed?

3. Do you feel excessively guilty over something(s) you've done in the past? If so, what?

Part XVII: Cursed objects

1. Do you have any idols, occult rings, or anything that could hold evil spiritual value in your home? If so, what? Any objects that hold evil spiritual value must be destroyed.

2. Do you have any gifts saved from sinful relationships? If so, explain. For example, if a man gives a woman a personal gift during an adultery that needs to be sold or destroyed.

Part XVIII: Severe trauma, abuse & disassociation

1. Have you ever been exposed to extreme abuse or a traumatic experience? Did it have a drastic effect on your emotional or mental system? If so, what happen? How did it affect you?

2. Have you ever disassociated or been diagnosed with Dissociative Identity Disorder (DID) or Multiple Personality Disorder (MPD)?

3. Are you aware of any alters (other personalities) that you may have? (If so, tell me about them)

4. Do you have a memory gap where you cannot remember a certain time of your life?

5. Do you have false memories of things that really didn't take place?

6. Have you ever been in a car accident or other traumatic situation? Have you ever witnessed a tragedy in real life?

Part XIX: Weaknesses

1. Do you struggle with any habitual sins? If so, what? Do you want to break those bad habits?

2. Do you struggle with any weaknesses such as lust, anger, hate, etc.? If so, what? Do you know where they came from or how they got started? Do you want to break free from those weaknesses?

Part XX: Pregnancy issues

1. Have you ever said something along the lines of, "I will never have children"?

2. Have you ever had an abortion or attempted one?

3. Have you ever had incest or ungodly sexual relations with somebody related to you? (See Leviticus 20:19-21, as this can cause a curse to land upon you which needs to be broken)

Part XXI: Other things to look for

1. Have you ever tried drugs? If so, how much, and how did it affect you? Why did you try drugs?

2. Have you ever thought about or attempted suicide?

3. Do you have any physical or mental disabilities, diseases or illnesses? Explain.

4. Do you want, and are willing to be delivered? Are you willing to give up those demon spirits and maybe make some lifestyle changes in order to keep your deliverance?

5. Do you experience unusual confusion settle upon you as you try to pray and read the Bible?

6. What kind of music do you like? (Please list all styles of music you currently enjoy, and give examples in each category you list, such as some names of artists and songs)

7. Have you previously enjoyed hard rock, metal, acid, alternative, rap, new age, or any other kind of worldly music? (Please provide some examples of artists and songs from each genre (type/style) of music you list)

8. Have you had any nightmares or weird experiences at night while supposedly sleeping?

9. Have you ever been in a trance or had an out of body experience?

10. Have you ever noticed time slipped right out from under you? For example, you look at your watch and its 7:00pm, then you look again what seemed like 15 minutes later and its 2:00am. This is a sign of a trance.

11. Have you ever touched or kissed a dead body? If so, explain whom and why and what happened afterwards.

12. Do you feel that you somehow have to earn your forgiveness? Do you 'wonder' if your sins are truly forgiven -- all of them? Are you aware of any signs of legalism or religious spirits operating in your mind?

13. Do you have any physical infirmities, sickness or diseases? If so, please list them.

14. Are you on any medications? If so, please explain.

15. Are you entertained by movies or TV shows which glorify death, murder, pain or suffering of others? Please explain.

16. Have you ever had any other kind of weird encounter with the spiritual realm?

Use this information to expose the root cause of the "it".

REFERENCES

1. Gary R. Collins, *Christian Counseling: A Comprehensive Guide*, 3rd Addition, Revised and Updated, NavPress, Colorado Springs, Colorado. ISBN 1418503290
2. Beilby, J.K. & P.R. Eddy. *Understanding Spiritual Warfare: Four Views*. Grand Rapids, Michigan: Baker, 2012.
3. Boyd, G.A., *God at War: The Bible and Spiritual Conflict*. Downers Grove, Illinois: IVP, 1997.
4. Hiebert, P. "Spiritual Warfare and Worldview"
5. Stedman, R.C, *Spiritual Warfare: Winning the Daily Battle with Satan.* Portland, Oregon: Multnomah, 1975.
6. Pirolo, N., *Prepare for Battle: Basic Training in Spiritual Warfare*, San Diego, California: Emmaus Road, International, 1997.
7. Arnold, E. C., *3 Crucial Questions about Spiritual Warfare*, Grand Rapids, Michigan: Baker, 1997.1
8. Rita Bennett, You Can Be Emotionally Free, 1982 ISBN 978 0 88270 748 8
9. Rita Bennett, Emotionally Free, 1982, ISBN 0 86065 194 0
   Publishers, PO Box 777,
10. Tonbridge, Kent TN 11 0ZS, England, 1997, reprinted 2004). ISBN 1-85240-110-9. (Available in the US through the Arsenal Bookstore, 11005 Voyager Parkway, Colorado Springs, CO 80921.)
11. John and Paula Sandford, Healing the Wounded Spirit (Victory House, 1985). ISBN 0-932081-14-2.
12. Norma Dearing, The Healing Touch (Chosen Books, 2002). ISBN 0-8007-9302-1. Charles Kraft, Deep Wounds, Deep Healing (Servant Pub., 1993). ISBN 0-89283-784-5.
13. Derek Prince, God's Remedy for Rejection (Whitaker House, 1993). ISBN 088368-864-6.
14. Francis and Judith MacNutt, Praying for Your Unborn Child (1989). ISBN 0-38523-2829. (Available from www.Christianhealingmin.org, 904-765-3332.)
15. Thomas Verney, MD, The Secret Life of the Unborn Child (Summit Books, 1981).
16. Anderson, Winning Spiritual Warfare 1990 ISBN 13: 978-0-89081-868-8 James
17. Friesen, Uncovering the Mystery of MPD, 1997 ISBN 1-56819-062-7
18. Diane Hawkins, Multiple Identities, 2009 ISBN 978-0-9708073-6-6,
19. Restoration in Christ Ministries, http://www.rcm-usa.org/index.htm
20. Francis MacNutt, Deliverance from Evil Spirits, 1995, 0-8007-9232-7, Chap 17, pp 223-235 (best introductory material)
21. Daniel Ryder, Breaking the Circle of SRA, 1992, 0-89638-258-3 (an excellent book by a Christian counselor)
22. Margaret Smith, Ritual Abuse, what it is, why it happens, how to help, 1993, 0-06-250214-X (in depth information about SRA and MPD)

23. The Christian Bible
24. The following associations focus on trauma and disassociation
    www.sidran.org, www.issd.org
25. Pentecost, J.D., *Your Adversary the Devil.* Grand Rapids, Michigan:
    Zondervan, 1969

About the Author
Dr. Paulette Douglas

Dr. Paulette Douglas truly epitomizes elegance in living a saved, sanctified and Holy life, set apart from the secular world! Dr. Douglas is an ordained minister with the Pentecostal Assemblies of the World, an anointed national and international Evangelist, teacher and preacher. Dr. Paulette Douglas is renowned for the ministry of exhortation to the Body of Christ through deliverance, inner healing, salvation and biblical counseling at seminars, prayer clinics, crusades and conferences. She has established three churches and assisted in establishing many other churches, ministries and colleges as she serves on the Body of Christ for Jesus. Dr. Douglas was baptized in the name of Jesus Christ and filled with the Holy Ghost in 1977. She was called to the ministry in 1981, taught bible study at Pacific Bell for nine years which established the Radiant Life in Christ Ministries. She was the founder and pastor of the Radiant Life in Christ Community Church in Baldwin Park, California for nearly four years. Dr. Douglas retired in 1996 with full benefits from AT&T after 26 years of service. God introduced Dr. Douglas to the LOVE and HERO of her life, Bishop Robert T. Douglas Sr. They were married, the ministries merged, and she became the First Lady of the Jacob's Ladder Family, the Women's Ministry Director, the Church Executive Administrator and the Dean of the California University of Theology. Dr. Robert and Paulette Douglas are the proud parents of three wonderful children, Shakinah, Robert Jr. and Sondra Imani. They are also blessed with two granddaughters, Demi and Rob'Ann (butter ball) four grandsons, Dylan, Dominick Terrell, the twins Canden and Caden. Seven Godchildren and twelve God -grandchildren. Dr. Douglas is a graduate from Fuller Theological Seminary, Pasadena, California, Pentecostal Bible College, Ministerial Training Institute of Inglewood, California and Aenon Bible College West Coast. She has a Bachelors degree in Biblical Studies, a Masters degree in Theology, a PhD in Theology, Administration and a PhD in Biblical Counseling. She has earned certificates from California Christian Leadership of Orange County in biblical counseling, Zoe Christian Leadership Training Institute, Church Growth International, Seoul Korea and School of World Missions and Evangelism, Los Angeles. Dr. Douglas is formerly the Dean/Professor of the Inglewood Ministerial Training Institute of Inglewood, the Inland Empire Ministerial Training Institute, the Tri-County Ministerial Training Institute (San Bernardino, Riverside and Los Angeles counties) and the Living Waters Bible College, Rialto California. Dr. Douglas is presently the Dean of Colleges and Professor for the California District Council Aenon Bible College and Institutes, the Jacob's Ladder California University of Theology and Aenon Bible Institute CDC Extension Campus in Inglewood, California and the American College Theological Seminary International University (ACTS). All schools are fully accredited institutions for pastors, evangelist, teachers and anyone who has the call of God on their lives for ministry. Dr. Douglas is currently the CDC International Missions President and the past Church/Extension/Evangelism/Altar Director for the California District Council of the Pentecostal Assemblies of the World, Inc. Past Evangelism President for the CHDC Area 2 and has worked with the PAW Evangelism Ministry for more than 35 years. Dr. Paulette Douglas is the published author of the book series "Get Rid of It before It Gets Rid of You". Self-Help Instructions on how to correct and receive deliverance in every area of your life. Dr. Douglas portrays tremendous strength and endurance in the Lord by jointly sharing the vision and love for God with Bishop Douglas. Her primary objective in life is to be that "Excellent Woman of God, walking in His Divine favor.

Books and Recourses Compiled by
Dr. Paulette Douglas

"How to Get Rid of "it", Before "it" Gets Rid of You" Series (12 Books on Self Deliverance)

Volume One- Healing and Deliverance from Additions

Volume Two- Healing and Deliverance from Sexual Additions

Volume Three- Healing and Deliverance from Personality Disorders

Volume Four- Healing and Deliverance from Negative Relationships

Volume Five- Healing and Deliverance Through Spiritual Warfare

Volume Six- Healing and Deliverance from Negatives Attitudes

Volume Seven- Healing and Deliverance from Success Hindrances

Volume Eight- Healing and Deliverance from Tormenting Emotions

Volume Nine- Healing and Deliverance from Spiritual Weakness

Volume Ten- Healing and Deliverance from Salvation Issues

Volume Eleven- Healing and Deliverance from Domestic Problems

Volume Twelve- Healing and Deliverance Through Biblical Counseling

How to Have an Anointed Altar Workers Ministry

How to Have an Effective Prayer and Fasting Life

How to Walk in Your Grace as the Wife of a Minister, Deacon, Pastor, or Bishop

How to be an Effective Life Coach